THE UNIVERSITY OF MICHIGAN
CENTER FOR CHINESE STUDIES

MICHIGAN PAPERS IN CHINESE STUDIES

Ann Arbor, Michigan

TWO TWELFTH CENTURY TEXTS ON CHINESE PAINTING

Translations of the Shan-shui ch'un-ch'üan chi
山水純全集　　by Han Cho 韓拙 and
Chapters Nine and Ten of Hua-chi 畫繼 by Teng Ch'un 鄧椿

by

Robert J. Maeda
Brandeis University

Michigan Papers in Chinese Studies

No. 8

1970

ISBN 0-89264-008-1

Printed in the United States of America

Contents

Introduction   1
     Notes   8

Part I: <u>Shan-shui ch'un-chüan chi</u>   10
     Notes   43

Part II: <u>Hua-chi</u>   53
     Notes   66

Introduction

These translations of the <u>Shan-shui ch'un-ch'üan chi</u>[1]
(preface dated 1121) by Han Cho[2] and chapters nine and ten of <u>Hua-chi</u>[3]
(preface dated 1167) by Teng Ch'un[4] originally formed one portion of a
doctoral dissertation in Fine Arts submitted to Harvard University
in 1969. My thesis subject was Academy landscape painting of the
twelfth century, particularly the transition between the Northern
and Southern Sung styles. As part of my research I focussed on these
two texts because both deal with the history and tenets of the Imperial
Painting Academy of Emperor Hui-tsung (reigned 1101-1126) in the
late Northern Sung period.

The Han Cho text is important because it is a model of
academic ideals, dated to the Hsüan-ho era (1119-1126), and because
it is by a reputed member of the Academy. In essence, it is a treatise
for beginning landscape painters, conservative in nature and not
specifically directed at Academicians. Teng Ch'un in his history of
painting titled <u>Hua-chi</u> is also concerned with the Academy but from
an historian's point of view.

Besides imparting insights into the taste and workings
of the Academy, both writers, historian and Academician, in ways
direct and indirect, show the influence of late Northern Sung literati
attitudes towards painting.

The primary biographical source for the author of the
<u>Shan-shui ch'un-ch'üan chi</u> is the epilogue appended to the text. It
was written by a certain Chang Huai 張懷 [5] and is dated December 5,
1121,some four months after the date of Han Cho's own preface to
the text (July 23, 1121). Although Chang Huai was familiar with Han
Cho and admired him, he does not provide much factual information.
He tells us that Han Cho was born in the Nan-yang district of Honan
province but does not give his birth date. During the Shao-sheng era
of Che-tsung's reign (1094-1097) he reports that Han Cho traveled
to the capital (K'ai-feng) where he entered the arts. He was favored
by the emperor's son-in-law, Chin-ch'ing (Wang Shen), who recommended
him to the imperial heir apparent, Hui-tsung. After Hui-tsung ascended
the throne, Han Cho was given the rank of <u>chih-hou</u> (official in waiting)

1

on the Calligraphy Board of the Han-lin Academy. He was then made a secretary on the History Board with a title of <u>chih chang</u> and a rank of <u>tai-chao</u> (official in attendance). At the time the epilogue was written, Han Cho had been granted the honorary title of <u>chung hsün lang</u>.

Further information about his social background and relative age when he wrote the treatise is supplied by Han Cho himself. He writes in his preface: "For generations, my family has been in the learned circle. I have been a petty official... From childhood I have been very fond of painting and even now that I have reached old age my interest in it has not flagged."

Yet, Han Cho's real identity, despite these facts, remains vague. There is ambiguity in the various editions of the text as to whether Han Cho was indeed a painter in Hui-tsung's Academy. [6] Even if he had been an unheralded member of that institution one might expect some mention of paintings by Han Cho in the <u>Hsüan-ho hua-p'u</u> (preface dated 1120) or <u>Hua-chi</u>, but none exist. This dearth of information may have led to the suggestion that Han Cho was actually Han Jo-cho 韓若拙 , a minor Academy painter of birds and portraits who was active during the same period. [7] Their contemporaneity and similarity in names[8] does not convince this writer of their oneness since Han Cho was first and foremost a landscape painter and according to Chang Huai was interested in no other subject. It seems more reasonable to assume that these were two different men living in the same period.

What is the basis for biographers placing Han Cho in Hui-tsung's Painting Academy? The answer, it seems, lies in an examination of the text.

There are several ways of examining the <u>Shan-shui ch'un-ch'üan chi</u>. First, one can read it simply as a manual for prospective landscape painters. As such, it would seem to be of limited value, especially to the modern reader. Why should a person interested in learning to paint landscapes read about the subject instead of turning his eyes upon nature itself. The Chinese painter, however, never did rely solely on his observation. What he saw in nature was always transformed into pictorial terms of "brush and ink" and was almost never a literal transcription of it. The one moment in Chinese painting history which is noted for the strict recording of nature is the period of Emperor Hui-tsung's Painting Academy in the late Northern Sung. In this regard, Sherman Lee and Wen Fong proposed a category which they called the "Literal style. " They wrote:

> It is as if the painters [of this style] thought
> to probe reality by taking a detail from a
> Monumental picture and examining it, part
> by part...[9]

In support of their interpretation of early twelfth century painting style, Lee and Fong use Han Cho's text as a literary parallel. Both its date, 1121, being coeval with that of the late Northern Sung Painting Academy, and its author, a purported member of it, seem to warrant such a conclusion. In his text, Han Cho presses points and leaves very little to the imagination, wanting no stone, as it were, left unturned. But this is as much a characteristic of his literary style as it is of a literal attitude about landscape painting. A great portion of his treatise could very well serve as a dictionary of landscape. Han Cho seems to have had as one of his main goals a listing of all landscape definitions and their practical application in painting.

Much of what Han Cho writes has been borrowed from previous writers although he does not hesitate to change or add to their words. His main sources are Chang Yen-yüan's Li-tai ming-hua chi (A. D. 847), Ching Hao's (late 9th, first half 10th c.) Pi-fa chi, Kuo Hsi's Lin-ch'üan kao-chih (1110?), and Kuo Jo-hsü's T'u-hua chien-wen chih (preface dated 1074). What differentiates the Ching Hao and Kuo Hsi texts from that of Han Cho is his organized and methodical approach compared to their often random, anecdotal, and allusive discussions. Han Cho is more blunt, taking the stance of a pedagogical sage. Since he wrote his work at a late stage of a life devoted to painting studies, his didacticism is perhaps excusable. As he also wrote in a period that saw the end of the first major style in the painting of landscape, his comprehensiveness is understandable.

In his attitude toward nature Han Cho can also be contrasted with Ching Hao and Kuo Hsi. He seems less interested in nature as such than he is in its depiction, i. e. painting. Unlike Ching Hao, he does not revel in the description of an actual landscape, nor does he give the same sense of ecstatic immersion in the scenery of a landscape painting as Kuo Hsi. His is a more detached, analytical view, that of an observer rather than a participant. While he is concerned with the minute details of nature he rails against the painter who would merely transcribe them into his painting. In this respect, he seems removed from the familiar stereotype of a painter in Hui-tsung's Painting Academy.

Thus, the "academic" character of the text is balanced by certain <u>wen-jen</u> tendencies. Han Cho's view of painting sometimes suggests what James Cahill wrote about Sung <u>wen-jen-hua</u>:

> As a worthy activity for the literatus. . . ,
> painting is now a means of self-cultivation;
> and the products of this activity, as embodiments
> of the admirable qualities of cultivated
> individuals, serve a Confucian end in
> conveying those qualities to others. [10]

By addressing his text to future scholars and including a chapter called "Concerning Ancient and Modern Scholars," Han Cho leaves little doubt that he considers painting a "worthy activity" for the cultivated man. His attachment to ancient standards and rules, distrust of skill and abhorrence of ostentation, regard for <u>li</u> ("right principle") in painting, as well as his belief in a kind of creative spontaneity all suggest the Confucian scholar rather than the Academician. Not that the two were incompatible necessarily; for as Cahill points out, the first chapter of the <u>Hsüan-ho hua-p'u</u> begins with a quotation from the <u>Analects</u> and indicates that Hui-tsung was not insensitive to the ideas of the <u>wen-jen</u>. [11]

In summation, the <u>Shan-shui ch'un-ch'üan chi</u>, with its rules and principles to guide the painter of landscape, can be considered an "academic" text representative of a Painting Academy such as Emperor Hui-tsung's. But in his connoisseurship and consciousness of the past Han Cho reveals an awareness perhaps of the innovative trends of the literati. In the context of painting history his text shows that the early twelfth century landscape painter had a long tradition to draw upon and if the tendency was toward a greater concentration in landscape designs --- this too may have been inevitable -- a reaction, as it were, to the crowded compositions which Han Cho

apparently favored. Han Cho, it is safe to say, comes at the
end of a particular landscape tradition --- that of Li Ch'eng and
Kuo Hsi --- and his text, in its codifying aims, marks the end
of that tradition in Sung painting literature.

The Hua-chi by Teng Ch'un is a text different in
motivation from the Shan-shui ch'un-ch'üan chi. It was written as
a sequel to two earlier painting histories, the T'ang dynasty
Li-tai ming-hua chi by Chang Yen-yüan and the eleventh century
T'u-hua chien-wen chih by Kuo Jo-hsü. The work is divided into
ten chapters and compiles facts and critical evaluations about
painters of the period from 1075 (the year following that given by
Kuo Jo-hsü as the terminal date of his history) to 1167, as well
as listings of selected masterpieces. His final two chapters which
I have translated deal with miscellaneous subjects from the distant
and recent past. [12]

As in Han Cho's case, biographical information about
Teng Ch'un is scarce. [13] He was born late in Northern Sung in
Shuang-liu in Szechwan. He came from a family of high officials although
Teng Ch'un himself held only a minor position as an assistant
sub-prefect (chün-shou).

Unlike Han Cho, Teng Ch'un gives us specific information
about the Imperial Painting Academy of Emperor Hui-tsung.
Writing from the perspective of a generation later, he discusses its
organization and examination system more objectively than he does
in describing the emperor and his paintings. [14] While he may have
been excessively fawning in his biography of the emperor he seems
to have caught precisely the mood and style of the Academy and its
painting. He points out that "form-likeness" and adherence to rules
were leading standards for painting in the Academy and these are
in keeping with Han Cho's attitudes. On the other hand, he agrees
with Kuo Jo-hsü that painting should transmit "soul," not just "form."
Han Cho also considered "form-likeness" as insufficient in capturing
a subject's inner reality.

Despite Teng Ch'un's acknowledgement of the talents of
painters who passed rigorous Academy examinations, his highest
praise is for painters of the aristocracy and of high official status.

In the beginning of chapter nine he makes clear the connection
between men of literature and painting and singles out as exemplars,
late Northern Sung literati, such as Su Tung-p'o, Mi Fei and
Li Lung-mien. In his words:

> They commented upon and classified works
> of art with purity and loftiness or they
> wielded the brush in an extraordinary and
> outstanding way.

Thus, as an historian, Teng Ch'un reported both the Establishment
values of the Academy and the intellectual tendencies of the wen-jen.
His own connoisseurship reflects, in spite of occasional lapses, the
highly critical spirit of a Mi Fei. Ironically, Mi Fei himself
does not escape Teng Ch'un's biting criticism.

In addition, Teng Ch'un offers miscellaneous information
about various painters (especially from his native Szechwan),
individual paintings (including those from foreign countries), and
connoisseurship. These fragments, plus the other remarks,
give us revealing glimpses of the personality and attitudes of the
twelfth century's chief historian of painting.

The Chinese editions of the texts which I used in my
translations were the following:

(1) Shan-shui ch'un-ch'üan chi

> In Hua-lun ts'ung-k'an, vol. 1, ed. Yü Hai-yen,
> Peking, 1962; also consulted: Mei-shu ts'ung-shu,
> II, No. 8, and IV, No. 10; and Shuo-fu and Wang-
> shih hua-yüan editions.

(2) Hua-chi

> In Hua-shih ts'ung-shu, vol. 1, ed. Yü Hai-yen,
> Shanghai, 1963; also consulted: Wang-shih
> hua-yüan edition.

In addition, I consulted the annotated Japanese versions
of the texts contained in Rekidai Garon[15] by Aoki Masaru and
Okumura Ikuryō. Without the aid of their notes to which I often
refer, the task of translating would have been infinitely harder.
Discrepancies among the texts are commented upon in my notes,
except when they are minor.

I would like to extend my sincere appreciation to Professor Max Loehr of Harvard University whose generous help and suggestions vastly improved these translations. I also wish to thank Professor Chun-shu Chang of the University of Michigan whose advice also sharpened the accuracy of my readings and Professor Richard Edwards, University of Michigan, for his encouragement and assistance in the publication of these texts. Finally, I offer these as "working translations" and whatever their shortcomings are my own responsibility.

Notes

1. The title of Han Cho's text, <u>Shan-shui ch'un-ch'üan chi</u>, has
   been variously translated. Nicole Vandier-Nicolas renders it:
   "Traité complet sur le paysage" in <u>Art et Sagesse en Chine</u>,
   Paris, 1963, p. 224. Roger Goepper titles it: "Collection
   of the Purity of Landscape" in <u>The Essence of Chinese Painting</u>,
   Boston, 1963, p. 10. Chang Huai in the epilogue attached to
   the Han Cho text writes: "...as Mr. Han Cho's painting was
   in harmony with the ancients and was unadulterated by later
   generations; hence, his essay collection is named 'ch'un-ch'üan'
   (purity)." Like Goepper, I would prefer to translate the title:
   "The Purity of Landscape Painting" or "The Essence of Landscape
   Painting," although the latter is not a literal translation.
   One must not overlook the fact that Han Cho's <u>tzu</u> was Ch'un-ch'üan,
   so that the title might be interpreted "Ch'un-ch'üan's Collected
   Essays on Landscape," although this does not seem to be
   correct.

2. <u>Tzu</u>: Ch'un-ch'üan, <u>hao</u>: Ch'in-t'ang.

3. Alexander C. Soper has translated the title as "More on Painting."
   See Soper, <u>Kuo Jo-hsü's Experiences in Painting</u> (<u>T'u-hua chien
   wen-chih</u>), Washington, 1951, p. xi.

4. <u>Tzu</u>: Kung-shou.

5. Chang Huai is otherwise unknown. Another name, Pang Mei
   邦美 , which follows that of Chang Huai at the end of the
   epilogue, may refer to an official named Shih Yen 時彥 , whose
   <u>tzu</u> was Pang Mei and who served in the Lung-t'u ko ("Dragon
   Picture Pavilion") of Hui-tsung's court. Whether Chang Huai
   and Pang Mei were the same person is not clear.

6. <u>Cf.</u> two editions of the text. (1) <u>Mei-shu ts'ung-shu</u>, II, epilogue:
   為直長秘書待詔 ("he was made a secretary on the History
   Board with the title of <u>chih-chang</u> and the rank of <u>tai-chao</u>").
   (2) MSTS, IV, epilogue: 為直長畫待詔 ("he was made a
   painter on the History Board with the title of <u>chih chang</u> and the
   rank of <u>tai-chao</u>"). Of the the two, the former version carries
   more logic as <u>chih chang</u> was the title of a subordinate officer
   of the History Board. As a landscape painter, however, Han
   Cho should normally have been associated with the Hua-yüan
   (Painting Academy). Neither Han Cho's text nor the Epilogue
   tell us this directly.

7. *Ssu-k'u ch'üan-shu tsung-mu t'i-yao*, reprinted in <u>Ssu-pu tsung-lu i-shu pien</u>. Shanghai, 1957, vol. 1, p. 723.

8. It should also be pointed out that Han Jo-cho was from Loyang, not Nan-yang, and that none of his biographical data match Han Cho's.

9. Sherman E. Lee and Wen Fong, <u>Streams and Mountains Without End</u>, Ascona, 1955, p. 23.

10. James F. Cahill, "Confucian Elements in the Theory of Painting," Essay contained in <u>Confucianism and Chinese Civilization</u>, ed. Arthur F. Wright, N.Y., 1964, p. 92.

11. Ibid., p. 100-101. Cf. Susan H. Bush who writes: "Hui-tsung himself painted ink birds and flowers in a scholarly mode" and "there is some evidence that scholar-officials and nobles shared a similar taste in art [in Hui-tsung's time]." See <u>The Chinese Literati on Painting: Su Shih (1037-1101) to Tung Ch'i-ch'ang (1555-1636)</u>, Harvard University Ph.D. thesis (unpublished), 1968, pp. 81-82.

12. Both chapters go under the general heading of "Tsa shuo" which Sirén translates as "Miscellaneous Sayings." See Osvald Sirén, <u>The Chinese on the Art of Painting</u>, N.Y., 1963, p. 88.

13. Biographical material on Teng Ch'un may be found in: <u>Ssu-pu tsung-lu i-shu pien</u>, op. cit., pp. 728b-729b; Teng Ch'un's own preface to <u>Hua-chi</u>; Friedrich Hirth, <u>Scraps from a Collector's Notebook</u>, Leiden, 1905, pp. 111-112.

14. Cf. <u>Hua-chi</u>, ch. 1.

15. Aoki Masaru and Okumura Ikuryō, <u>Rekidai Garon</u>, Tokyo, 1942, pp. 91-160.

...in *Lungs... Chan luh*, 1947, vol. 7, p. 156.

It should also be pointed out that the journey from Chang-an to Shang-yang... and that... one... date... mathematical date match...

Bernard S., *Leaders and... literature and socialism without...*, 143, p. 22.

Thomas Ernhill, "Confucian Elements in the Taiping Rebellion," essay contained in *Confucianism and Chinese Civilization*, edited by A. Wright, N. Y., 1964, p. 27.

Ibid., p. 160-61. "Christ was the... Each was a filial son and a loyal subject; lily pads and flowers... to a brotherhood and... should... forsake...

...somewhat similar treatment (in literary terms)... and Lin Chinese Literature on Political... from... to Ting... *Chinese*... Harvard University, 1958, pp. 31-38.

...improve number... prepared it... translated as "imperial son..."... *Chinese literary... in...*, p.

...Deprived deliberately of a China source... such his the image is... *Pao Chao and... Tu-fu*, Doctoral dissertation, Harvard University, Department of..., 1968, p. 1-17, 63.

World History and Quotations from... Group, Press, 1949, pp. 23-24.

Part I

Shan-shui ch'un-ch'üan chi

By Han Cho

Han Cho's <u>Preface</u>[1]

Now, [the art of] painting was, after Fu Hsi had drawn up
the eight trigram images,[2] [the method] through which one mastered
the [moral] virtues of the universe and symbolized the nature of all
things. Subsequently, in the period of the Yellow Emperor, Shih
Huang and Ts'ang Chieh[3] were born. Shih Huang drew the shapes of
fish, dragon, tortoise, and bird. Ts'ang Chieh took these shapes and
constructed [written] characters from them. Gradually, through
transmission and change of these shapes and characters, pictures and
writings were developed. Writing originated from drawing [delineation]
--- that is, drawing came first and writing followed.

Tradition says: "Painting perfects culture, helps in moral
obligations, probes into divine permutations, plumbs deep and recondite
things, has the same merits as each of the Six Classics and is in harmony
with the passage of the four seasons. It arose from nature and was
not created by man. Writing and drawing/delineation [before Ts'ang
Chieh's time] were the same and were not differentiated. Still, it was
known that though writing was able to describe things, it was unable
to record their forms, and that characters had nothing in them whereby
they could reveal form [while] drawing was unable to express the
[meaning of] words. To preserve form there was nothing better than
drawing, but to record speech there was nothing better than writing.
In short, though writing and drawing were different in name, they were
considered to be the same in method/principle."[4]

The ancients said: "painting is measurement,"[5] but it is more
than that. With it, one can probe into anything within the universe,
manifest what is not illumined by the sun and moon. By wielding a fine-
tipped brush one can reveal a myriad things from one's mind. By
exercising one's abilities one can create a thousand <u>li</u> within the palm of one
hand. Is it anything but the brush, then, that completes what has been
created [by nature]?

Since ancient times the most refined art of enlightened scholars
has been painting. Accordingly, there ought to be a great many who are
skilled in painting. For generations, my family has been in the learned
circle. I have been a petty official. But my disposition is undisciplined
and unrefined. However, my bent is always toward a fondness of painting.

I seek out as models intelligent men of the past, and investigate
the "dregs" of ancient and modern times. From childhood
I have been very fond of it and even now that I have reached old age
my interest in it has not flagged; I am afraid only that the time that
I have spent on learning [the art of painting] is quite limited and my
work is too amateurish.

However, this is all due to my inborn characteristic!
Wang Wei of the T'ang dynasty as a writer overshadowed his
generation; as a painter excelled those of past and present. Once
he inscribed his own [painting], writing: "The present age errs in
taking me to be a poet; in a former life I must have been a painter. "[6]
How true are these words!

The art of painting landscape has purity and blandness in its
character, subtlety and profundity in its order. As for the infinite
ways of representing scenery of the four seasons and windy and rainy
weather, these are entirely dependent on ink and brush. As to the
exhaustive research into the subtleties and profundities of the art of
painting, unless one is an erudite man, how can one deeply understand
the marvelous uses of painting? However, there are quite a few
unlearned and ordinary men who neglect these doctrines. Those whose
scholarship is broad are anxious not to fall into superficiality and
pettiness. They who tirelessly struggle for wealth and fame simply
have principles and goals different from mine --- they are beneath
our notice!

I have gathered together landscape and figure paintings and
made a collection of them for a long time now. From the characteristics
of those landscapes I intend to discuss, in a general way, painting rules.
course] I do not presume to make any lofty commentary; but even if
my words are graceless, they may perhaps provide future scholars
with an opportunity for enlightenment. Accordingly, I will discuss
[these matters] in the following ten chapters.[7] Hsüan-ho, hsin-ch'ou,
last month of summer, eighth day (July 23, 1121).[8]

Concerning Mountains

Generally, one speaks of painting mountains in terms of measurement - which was Wang Wei's rule.[9] Mountains are arranged in a principal-auxiliary, superior-inferior order and are in accord with the contrasting dualities of <u>Yin</u> and <u>Yang</u> (Earth and Heaven). Each mountain has its own form and designation. The scholar who is practiced in landscape painting and loves study, will have to know these [rules].

The principal mountain is the tall, large one within a group. It is heroic and estimable, and is surrounded by supporting peaks.

The large mountains are the superior ones, the smaller are inferior.

It is proper that the large and small hills and mounds be arranged [in such a manner] that they are facing front in courtly obeisance; those that are not are improper. The auxiliary mountains are neither subservient nor haughty.

To distinguish light and shade use ink [in such a way as] to obtain separation between rich and dilute. Concave [areas] are dark. Convex [surfaces] are light.

In mountains there is an order of precedence according to height and size. Painting gradually from the near to the far, one finally comes to painting the most imposing mountains.

Hung-ku-tzu (Ching Hao) wrote: "The pointed [mountains] are called peaks; the levelled ones are called plateaus; and the rounded ones are called conical peaks. The connected ones are called ranges. The mountain that has caves is called <u>hsiu</u>岫; the steep walls are called precipices and below the precipices are grottoes."[10] Below these grottoes are caves which are called rocky caves.

A mountain which is big and high is called lofty; small but high ones are called steep (sharp).

A sharply pointed mountain is a tall but slender and steep one.

Low, tapering ones are broad in appearance.

Small mountains assembled together are called <u>lo-wei</u> 羅圍.

Triple mountain ranges are called <u>hsi-she</u> 襲涉. A double mountain is called <u>tsai-mu-ying</u> 再木映. A single-[layered] mountain is termed <u>p'ei</u> 伾.

Small mountains are called <u>chi</u> 岌, and a larger one is called <u>huan</u> 峘.

<u>Chi</u> 岌 are said to be excessively tall.

Mountains that are joined together are called "connected mountains" (<u>shu-shan</u> 屬山).

Mountains that are connected in an unbroken chain are called a range (<u>i</u> 嶧). Such mountains surpass [in length] massed mountains that are joined.

Those mountains which are long and have a ridge are called <u>shan-kang</u> 山岡 .

The slope near the top of a mountain is called "blue-green" (<u>ts'ui-wei</u> 翠微).

The peak of a mountain range in <u>shan tien</u> 山巔 .

<u>Yen</u> 岩 is a cave.

A cave that contains water is called <u>tung</u> 洞 (grotto) and one without water is called <u>fu</u> 府 .

A hall-shaped mountain is called <u>t'ang</u> 堂 .

A mountain which is like a screen is called <u>chang</u> 嶂 .

Small mountains which lie between large mountains but are not connected to them are called <u>hsien</u> 鮮 .

Connected mountains which are broken off are called "broken-off view" (<u>chüeh-ching</u> 絕景).

A mountain which is pressed between the right and left ⌈banks of a river⌉ is called wu 屋.

A multitude of small rocks is called ai 磴 ("stumbling stones").

Dish-like rocks are p'ing shih 平石 ("flat rocks").

A mountain with much vegetation is called hu 岵 ; one without vegetation is called kai 垓.

Rocks which are covered with earth are called ts'ui-wei 崔嵬 ; in other words, there is earth on top of the rocks.

Earth which is covered with rocks is called ch'u 岨 ; in other words, there are rocks on top of the earth.

An earth mound is called fu 阜.

A slope is called a p'o 坡.

A high plain is called lung 壠.

In hill and mountain ranges are hidden and exposed forests and springs and a gradual distinction betweeen far and near.

As for valleys, a valley with a thoroughfare is called ku 谷; one which is unsuitable for a thoroughfare is ho 壑 (gulley).

Ch'iung-tu 窮瀆 ("dried-up ditch") is a valley where nothing passes through; but a valley with a stream flowing is ch'uan 川 .

Water which courses between two mountains is called chien 澗 (mountain torrent); water which trickles between mounds is called ch'i 溪 (creek).

In the midst of ch'i 谿 (deep gorge) there is water. [11]

It is proper to paint water that winds and turns, is hidden, then exposed to view; continues on unseen and is later seen again.

    The mountains of the four quarters have a character and
scenery each of which is different. The eastern mountains are
staunch and broad, their appearance is massive and their water is
scarce. The western mountains have river gorges and steep rising
hills; the mountains are lofty and dangerous. The southern mountains
are low and small and water is plentiful; the river and lake scenery
is luxuriant and flourishing. The northern mountains are broad and
spread out and there are many hills. The forests are thick but
the streams are narrow. In the eastern mountains it is fitting to depict
villages, wood gatherers, farmers, inns, mountain dwellings,
government officials and wayfarers. In the western mountains it is
fitting to apply cities and suburbs, plank roads, fowlers' nets, tall
pavilions, and Taoist temples. In the northern mountains it is fitting
to apply transport carts, camels, and fuel-gatherers carrying loads
on their backs. In the southern mountains it is fitting to apply river
areas, fish markets, lakeside villages, and mountainous suburbs.
But if you add rice fields and angling pleasures you should not use
transport carts and camels. It is necessary to know that northern
and southern habits differ and that these are profound differences.

    Mountains have four seasonal aspects. Spring mountains
are beautiful and seductive, as if smiling; summer mountains are
bluish-green, as if dripping [with dew]; autumn mountains are bright
and clean, as if washed; and winter mountains are pale and bleak, as
if sleeping. These comments have been made about the moods of the
four seasons. [12] Kuo Hsi says: "There are three [modes of rendering]
distance in [painting] mountains; looking up at mountains from below
and seeing in the background faintly-colored mountains is called
'high distance;' looking from the front of mountains and observing
the mountains behind is called 'deep distance;' looking from a near
mountain to a neighboring, lowlying mountain is called 'level distance.'"
I have a further theory about the three distances. From a nearby
shore of a broad body of water [to see] far-reaching, distant mountains
is what I call "broad distance;" when there are mists and fog that are
vast and boundless so that wilderness and sea appear indistinct, this
is called "shrouded distance;" and scenery which is incomplete
(cut off), vague and misty is called "dark distance." [13]

    In regard to the celebrated appearances of the mountains
mentioned above they should be noted in the practice of painting; at
the same time they should provide answers for the learned and accomplishe
man's questions. If a man is asked about these matters and cannot
reply he will be thought an ignorant man. He [simply] has to know.

Moreover, in poetry there may occur the names of all the mountains,
but even if one knows their names but does not know their appearance,
how can one set the hand to composing them?

In paintings of panoramic landscapes, mountains are placed
in ranges one above the other; even in one foot's space they are
deeply layered; from the far to the near [rows] or from the bottom
to the top layers the mountains are distributed in support of each other,
and proper order is adhered to by first arranging the venerable
mountains followed by the subservient ones. However, [compositions]
should not be too crowded. It is essential that mountain vapors and
mists cut down/cancel the sunlight, and that forests cover [the mountain].
One should not expose the body [of the mountain] as if it were a
person without clothes. Then they would be poor/impoverished mountains.
For the forests [of a mountain] are its clothes, the vegetation its
hair, the vapor and mists its facial expressions, the scenic elements
its ornaments, the waters its blood vessels, the fog and mists its
expressions of mood.[14]

In painting, if a person does not seek out the ancient methods
he cannot portray the true mountain; he will merely pursue the
common and transient, selecting and combining the empty and frivolous;
furthermore, by conceitedly thinking himself superior to past and
present, he deceives himself; he changes right to wrong. Such a man
is dull, and ignorant of landscape's essentials. It would be very
difficult to converse with him. Alas! Of contemporaries, few are
right, many are wrong; they seize what is new and neglect the old ---
because of the seductive grasps of profit. Scholars who have a broad
knowledge of antiquity and even so have a liking for present [scholarship]
are rare indeed. If there is anyone who has mastered these profound
principles, then you can certainly discuss these matters with him.
As for those who laugh at the past and are proud of the present and
ridicule learned scholars, they would consider these words of mine
merely as a joke.

Concerning Water

Water has aspects of sluggishness or swiftness, shallowness or depth --- these are its main features.

Water [which accumulates] on the top of a mountain is called chien 涀; it is water which issues from high mounds.

The water [which accumulates] at the bottom of a mountain is called ch'an 潺; it is water forming gently moving ripples.

The water of a mountain torrent is called p'eng-t'uan 澎湍. However, [water] which scours rocks is called yung-ch'üan 湧泉 ("bubbling spring").

Water which leaps and gushes out from between rocky gorges is called p'en-ch'üan 噴泉 ("spurting spring").

A p'u-ch'üan 瀑泉 is a stream of water which cascades from between high cliffs like a thousand feet of glossy silk thread and splashes into the unfathomable depths below, where it seethes and swirls with such frightening billows and angry waves that even fish and turtles are unable to live there.

Chien-p'u 濺瀑 ("splashing cascade") is water which has accumulated in mountains and which wishes to flow out from its rocky barriers. Through crevices it furiously descends, its shattering waves are like boiling water. As for the rocks which it strikes and flows over --- their edges are smooth and rounded. [Finally], it joins together, blending into one stream. [15] Through the use of brush tone (literally: "lightness and heaviness") one can distinguish between aspects of depth or shallowness, or what is full and what is scattered.

When swift currents converge and collide, creating a violently resounding choppy torrent, the crash of the water as it converges from every direction is like the sound of thunder and wind. This sound is called ch'uang 潒.

What is called <u>i-shui</u> 沂水 is water which in one undivided
stream flows downward; compared with the <u>p'u-ch'üan</u> [see above]
it is rather different and should be distinguished.

As for sea water, its wind and waves are big and vast, and
its great billows turn and toss. In landscape painting it is rarely used.

<u>Hsia-shui</u> 硤水 is a swift (so swift that boats cannot stop
on it), arrow-like, current which runs between two dangerous
precipices (so steep they cannot be scaled). There is no water faster
than this.

What is called the Chiang-hu 江胡 (the [Yangtze] river)
flows into the vastness of Lake Tung-t'ing 洞庭 .

<u>Ch'üan-yüan</u> 泉源 (spring) is water which flows out constantly.
Since such water flows copiously and continuously, Mencius said:
"There is a spring of water; how it gushes out! It rests not day nor
night."[16]

As for streams **one** should use them **often** in landscapes;
they should be painted as they wind and turn, are hidden, then exposed
to view; continue on unseen and are later seen again. From faraway
to near they should be enveloped and hidden in mists and haze to
make them beautiful. When Wang Yu-ch'eng (Wang Wei) said:
"Roads that seem about to end but do not end, streams that seem about
to flow but do not flow,"[17] isn't this perhaps what he meant?

<u>Sha-ch'i</u> 砂磧 are sandbanks which are in the middle of a
stream of adverse currents. As the water flows around both banks,
it quickens and there is a sound.

<u>Shih-ch'i</u> 石磧 are stones which support the banks of a
stream and obstruct the current. The water which flows along the
two banks swirls about in ripples around the stones.

Where there is a bank but no water is called <u>ho</u> 壑 (gulley).

Now, water has four seasonal aspects and these follow
seasonal weather conditions. Spring water is subtly green, summer
water is subtly cold, autumn water is subtly clear and winter water
is subtly melancholy.

20

The island and the misty islet are places in the midst of water where people can live and scenery is concentrated.

When it comes to subjects for painting such as swift rivers where fish can be caught or large ponds where geese abound, and so forth, there are many who take pleasure in painting them and who thereby manifest their talent.

Moreover, since water is a mountain's arteries, when painting it, one should paint the sky high and the water broad in order to make a beautiful [painting].

Concerning Forests
and Trees

A forest has seasonal periods of luxuriance and decline, denseness and thinness. In just an inch of space, a painter can represent its richness and compactness, and distinguish between forests that are near and far. Old trees are venerated for their height and stateliness, hoary antiquity, strength and toughness, and are depicted with strong and heavy brushstrokes. In the depiction of an elegant or plain tree the brushstrokes should thicken and thin. Furthermore, the depiction of a light (weight) or heavy tree lies in the use of brush. High or low tones for shading are entirely dependent on the use of ink. These are essentials for painting the category of forests and trees.

Hung-ku-tzu (Ching Hao) wrote in his treatise: "Brushwork has four aspects: muscle, bone, skin, and flesh. Strokes which are cut off but whose force/impetus is uninterrupted are called 'muscle.' Strokes that are tied to the bones are called 'skin.' Brushstrokes which are firm and straight and expose the joints are called 'bones.' Strokes that thicken and thin, that are round and plump are called 'flesh.' In particular, one ought to paint the bones and flesh as being interdependnet. Excessive flesh results in fleshiness and weakness; if too soft and seductive, bone is wanting. Excessive bone results in stiffness and woodenness; if there is muscle to excess, flesh in wanting. If strokes are fragmented/broken off, muscle in wanting. When ink is used in a broad and simple manner, truth is lost; when ink is used in too delicate and timid a manner, it impairs the right appearance."[18]

Trees must be well-proportioned and possess strength. They should not be too tall/long or else they will lose their aspect of strength. They should not be too short either for then they will become vulgar and commonplace. It is from having these aspects that trees derive their strength. Trees without these aspects are formless and twisted and deficient in strength. But if a tree is merely stiff and hard and has no turns or twists, then it is deficient in vitality. If the brushwork is too finicky and the ink[19] too sparing, then the trees are weak. In a general way, I agree with these useful rules.

We venerate trees which are green and vigorous or old and rigid. Their shapes are numerous. Some trees stretch out high their soaring branches; some twist and turn, bending up and down; some bend their trunks as if they were bowing; some are like drunken men wildly dancing; some are like [men] with dishevelled hair grasping swords --- all of these are pine trees. Furthermore, some pine trees have aspects like angry dragons or frightened young dragons; some have forms like ascending dragons or like crouching tigers; some appear to be wild and strange and some buoyant and graceful; some seem proud and haughty; some humble and modest; some spread out and lean over a bank as if to drink from the middle of a stream;[20] some lean over from precipices of lofty mountain ranges, their trunks overturning; these being the manner of pines whose aspects are manifold, and transformations inestimable.[21]

In painting tree roots, those trees which lean and rise at river banks have roots which seem to rise and fall, as they push the earth away. They are unrestrained and scattered. But as for ordinary standing trees, one should paint them with large trunks deeply embedded in the ground. Nearby, scatter small roots which are about to come out of the earth.

In painting withered trees and branches, one simply must pay attention to their hollows and sunken cavities.

Again, pine trees are like noblemen; they are the elders among the trees. Erect in bearing, tall and superior, they reach into the sky. Their authority extends to the Milky Way. Their branches scatter and hang over. Below, they welcome the common trees. With reverence they regard those inferiors, like the virtue of the gentleman whose conduct should be catholic and not partisan.[21a] Ching Hao said: "The [pine] trees that formed the grove were vigorous and tall of trunk; those not of the grove held themselves in restraint and bowed in natural submission."[22] There are those which bend down and shade and whose branches coil, whose heads droop over and whose waists are twisted --- these are peculiar pines. Those that have old bark, green scales, withered branches, and few needles are old pines. Wang Wei said: "Pine trees are not to be distinguished from elder brother and younger brother,"[23] which means their rank/position should be in accord with their inferiors; likewise, he said: "There are children and grandchildren," which means those that have new branches added on are young pines. Their twigs/tips tower aloft, rising upward; their needles intertwine and their shade is great.

Moreover, a cedar tree is like a marquis. The [Wang Wei] treatise also says: "Cedar [branches] grow downward in great luxuriance; they must be extremely expansive and flourishing;"[24] as for those whose bark is fittingly twisted, have knots streaked with lines, have many branches but few leaves, knotholes that are hollow, whose aspect is like a scaly dragon, body twisting and turning, agitatedly changing position in perverse ways --- they are the forms of old cedars. As for young cedars, their leaves are dense, their branches spread out and their twigs rise up.

The cypress tree has a trunk like a pine and the bark of a cedar[24a] and is combined into a <u>sung-po</u> (松柏 "pine-cedar"). Hence, it is named <u>kuei</u> 檜. As for those whose branches horizontally stretch out and coil and wind, whose leaves are scattered and in disarray, they are of the class of old cypress.

It would be difficult to discuss completely the remaining species of trees. [I wish to mention] only the <u>ch'iu</u> 楸 (catalpa), <u>wu</u> 梧 (sterculia platanifolia), <u>huai</u> 槐 (locust), and <u>liu</u> 柳 (willow). All are different in shape and manner.

Generally, those that are leafy trees are venerated for their abundant and dense foliage. But when it comes to a winter forest, it is essential that its groves rise up in deep layers; that they be dispersed but not scattered. Furthermore, one ought to compose withered twigs and old felled trees [in these wintry scenes], and in the background use thin ink to paint secondary kinds of trees. If you do all these things in a harmonious manner, then a lonely, expressive mood of purity will be obtained.

Forest intervals should not be left blank. Particularly, one should paint mists which shed light all around. Certainly, it was Hsien-hsi (Li Ch'eng) who was deeply accomplished in these marvelous practices.

Yüan Ti of Liang wrote: "Trees have four seasonal aspects; in spring they blossom, in summer they give shade, in autumn their hair [falls], in winter their bones [show]."[25]

"In spring they blossom" means that the leaves are delicate and the flowers numerous; "in summer they give shade" means that the leaves are thick and luxuriant; "in autumn their hair [falls]" means that the leaves loosen and gracefully fall; "in winter their bones [show]" means that the branches wither and the leaves dry up. He mentions the category of forested mountain peaks --- which means there are close-knit trees on the tops of mountain precipices. There is the forested foothill category --- which means the forest at the foot of a mountain. There is the distant forest category --- which means distant forests in misty darkness.[26]

As for distant trees[27] one should select their general appearance but one should not portray them recklessly slanting or in an upside-down/confused manner, but rather show them minute in scale, pale in color, standing erect, differentiating their form so that each one is distinct. It is further said that as for disposition, form provides it.[28] In capturing the general appearance of miscellaneous [grouped] trees, use dots of ink applied lightly and evenly.

Forests are mountain's clothes. As in the case of people, to be without clothes causes a mountain to not have a properly flourishing appearance. Hence, we venerate [mountains] with dense forests and luxuriant trees because they have a gloriously thriving appearance. [A mountain] with few trees is called lu-ku 露骨 ("bare bones"). It is like a person with few clothes. But if one is painting just one tree and one rock, then it is absolutely necessary to simplify.

Concerning Rocks

In depicting rocks, we admire massiness and diversity, virile boldness, hoary hardness and roughness; [there are rounded boulders called] alum heads, and [rocks with] rhombic faces; rocks piled up --- some thick, some thin, or pressed down into thick layers. Use ink to bring out their firmness and solidity, their concavities and convexities. Brush in <u>ts'un</u> (texturing) in light and dark tones, and then dot the rocks evenly with tones of high to low intensity. Such are the effects of <u>p'o-mo</u> 破墨 (broken ink).[29]

Large, flat rocks are called <u>p'an-shih</u> 盤石 . Yet, rocks do not have but one appearance --- some are piled up but are refined and smooth in appearance. Some rocky summits are extremely dangerous looking. There are precipices with irregular outlines; peculiarly shaped rocks which have tumbled down from above. There are some which are immersed in water and whose depth cannot be fathomed. Some have only their bases submerged but they are supported by other rocks. As for mountain peaks that are precipitous and jagged --- in a myriad wondrous ways they spread out horizontally and vertically --- their shapes are unlimited.

In addition, there are various kinds of texture strokes (<u>ts'un</u>). There is the <u>p'i-ma ts'un</u> 披麻皴 (hemp fiber <u>ts'un</u>),[30] the <u>tien-ts'o ts'un</u> 點錯皴 (ornamental dot <u>ts'un</u>), the <u>cho-t'a ts'un</u> 斫嵯皴 (cutting mountain <u>ts'un</u>), the <u>heng-ts'un</u> 橫皴 (horizontal <u>ts'un</u>), and the <u>yün erh lien shui ts'un</u> 勻而連水皴 (uniform and connected water <u>ts'un</u>). For each of these strokes and dots there are ancient and modern schools, a number of whose rules still exist.

The ancients said: "Rocks [seen] ten paces away lose their true appearance, while mountains even ten <u>li</u> away possess it."[31] Moreover, rocks being of the same substance as mountains, one should venerate their quality of <u>ch'i-yün</u> 氣韻 but not their <u>k'u-tsao</u> 枯燥 (lifeless) quality. When painting rocks, do not depart from these views.

Concerning Clouds and Mist,

Misty Luminosity, Wind, Rain, Snow and Fog

As for the atmosphere pervading the mountains and rivers, the clouds are most important. Clouds proceed from the deep valleys and end in the land in the east (yü-i 嵎夷).[32] They obscure the sun and conceal the sky and are limitless and unfixed. Rising and clearing the skies they manifest the ch'i 氣 of the four seasons; spreading and darkening the atmosphere they follow the disposition of the four seasons. Thus, spring clouds are like white cranes; their aspect is modest and reserved; peacefully they stretch out. Summer clouds are like strange peaks; their aspect is dark and melancholy; heavy or thin, shining or somber, their aspects vary. Autumn clouds are like light waves, they float in fragments like cotton (tou-lo 兜羅) --- serene and pure white. Winter clouds done with limpid ink are dark and gloomy --- revealing [this season's] mysterious and dark aspect, when darkness and cold are extremely severe. These are the appearances of fair weather clouds during the four seasons.

In respect of cloudy weather --- spring clouds are thin and rippled; summer clouds abruptly darken; autumnal clouds lightly float; winter clouds are sadly pale. These are the appearances of cloudy weather during the four seasons.

However, the substance of a cloud coalesces and dissolves differently. When it is light, it is mist. When it is heavy, it is fog. When it floats, it is a fair-weather cloud. When it condenses, it is steamy vapors. In addition to these, there is the appearance of mountain mist, which consists of a vaporous lightness. Clouds curl up and mists stretch out. In short, clouds are vapors which have condensed.

Generally, in painting, one should distinguish between climatic [conditions]; chief among these is differentiating between clouds and mists. As for those that are used in landscape painting --- do not heavily apply colors to mists; do not use bright colors on clouds. By doing so, there is the danger of losing the misty luminosity, the rustic nature, and natural appearance.

Among clouds there are such distinctions as floating clouds, clouds which emerge from valleys, wintry clouds and evening clouds.

Ranking next to clouds is fog (wu 霧), which includes such categories as dawn fog, distant fog, and wintry fog.

Next to fog there is the categoy of vapors (yen 烟), among which are morning vapors, evening vapors and light vapors.

Next to vapors there is the category of hanging mist (ai 靄), which includes river mist, evening mist and distant mist.

Outside of these four categories (cloud, fog, vapors, hanging mist) is another, which is called rosy clouds (hsia 霞). Sunrise (eastern glow) is called ming-hsia 明霞 ("morning's rosy clouds"); sunset (western glow) is called mu-hsia 暮霞 ("evening's rosy clouds"), but these are just single periods of atmospheric brilliance in the morning and evening. One should not use them often.

In general, the five preceding categories make up the misty luminosity of a mountain's appearance and are the adornments of distant mountain tops and distant trees. If you are good at painting these [atmospheric effects] then you can capture the true atmosphere/ spirit of the four seasons and the marvelous principles of nature. Hence, one cannot ignore the effects of misty luminosity in landscape painting as they are in accord with its natural laws.

Although the wind has no [observable] form, the forms of grasses, trees, clothes and scarves, cloud tops and hanging rain clouds have not the slightest opposition to it [i.e. they reveal its effect]. If they opposed it, then you would lose its essence.

To continue, I shall take up the occasions of rain and snow, even though their seasons are different. As for rain, there is "driving rain," "showers," "night rain," "threatening rain," and "clearing after rain." As for snow, there is "wind driven snow," "river snow," "night snow," "spring snow," "evening snow," "threatening snow," and "clearing after snow."

Generally, the prospect of rain or snow is based on the lightness or heaviness of the clouds[33] or judged by the wind's velocity. Only by considering such weather conditions can one apply the brush. Since it is through the appearance of clouds that one can determine[34] the likelihood of rain or snow, they should be dark [in both cases] and not light.

Furthermore, the Erh ya 爾雅 [35] says: "Heaven's vapors which descend but to which earth does not respond are called meng 霿 (mist)," which means a dark but light [in weight] substance; "earth's vapors which ascend but to which heaven does not respond are called wu 霧 (fog), which means a dark and heavy substance.

When the wind and rain is intense,[36] then it is impossible to distinguish far from near.

When cold winds are strong and it is dark,[37] then it is impossible to distinguish mountains from forests.

All of these are unseasonal phenomena and should not be included in the same classification as clouds.[38]

As for [clouds resembling] the forms of fish, dragon, and grassy vegetation, it was the Lü Shih [Ch'un Ch'iu's] 呂氏 [春秋][39] words which were very clear on this subject. As for [analogies] to the shapes of the soaring luan bird 鸞 and the flying phoenix, it was Mr. Lu Chi's 陸機 discussion[40] which was profoundly enlightening. But when probing into the subtleties of nature's laws and investigating the effects of wind and snow: is it possible not to go deeply into these matters?

Concerning Figures, Bridges, Gateways,

Walls, Temples, Monasteries, Mountain Retreats,

Boats, and Scenes of the Four Seasons

Whenever painting figures, one should not use coarse,
vulgar types but venerate those that are pure and elegant and in
lonely retirement. As they are proud retired officials dwelling
in seclusion they are different in body and appearance from village
dwelling old peasants and fishermen. Taking a glance at the figures
in the landscapes of antiquity, they really are men of leisure and
refinement; there are none who are vulgar or hateful. As for
recent productions they are frequently coarse and vulgar, extremely
wanting in the ancients' attitudes.

As for bridges called ch'iao 橋 and chou 杓, a bridge
beneath which boats pass is called ch'iao; one under which boats
cannot pass is called chou.[41] The latter is a bridge whose horizontal
beams are laid across a mountain torrent. Only people on foot can
cross it.

As for gateways --- they are located in a mountain gorge.
There is only one road leading through. With not even a small
stream running near it, it really serves only as a gateway.

As for city walls --- their battlements are successively
aligned, their towers are mutually facing; they must encircle the
area between the mountains and the forests. They should not be
completely exposed to view lest the painting should be classified
as a [geography] book illustration. In landscape painting only
ancient battlements should be used.

In painting Buddhist temples and Taoist monasteries ---
they should be horizontally tucked in among remote valleys, distant
cliffs, and steep precipices.

Only pennant-carrying wine shops and inns should be placed
along the roads between the villages.

With regard to the mountains where dwell recluses and retired officials, it is absolutely necessary that they be lonely places.

Where there are broad areas of land, one should paint thatched cottages and houses, peaceful forests, oxen and horses, and farmers.

Where there are broad areas of water, one should paint fish markets and fish ponds, as well as fishermen, water-chestnut gatherers, and nets drying in the sun.

Speaking of boats, a large one is called <u>chou</u> 舟 and a small one is called <u>ch'uan</u> 船 .

A <u>t'ing</u> 艇 is what a fisherman boards; a <u>ch'uan</u> 船 is what a recluse boards.

Some boats are fitted with nets and cages; some drag after them fishing lines --- they are termed <u>yü-t'ing</u> 漁艇 (fishing boats).[42]

Some boats are wooden house boats. Some are made with awnings and curtains and are <u>yu-ch'uan</u> 遊船 (excursion boats).

A boat that is rowed with small oars is called a <u>fei-hang</u> 飛航

A boat that has been hollowed out of a single log is called <u>hsiang-ts'ao</u> 相槽 (double-grooved).

The kind of boats that should be used in landscape painting are those that travel the waves floating lightly. They should not be heavily laden. As for other heavily laden river and sea boats, they should be sparingly used in landscape painting.

In classifying the scenes of the four seasons it is absolutely necessary to be clear on nature's laws and rules regarding human activity. Pictures of spring should be painted with figures that are happy and at ease --- those that walk on the green (in the) suburbs; saunter along the green paths; compete at the rope swing. Depict fishermen singing, ferry boats crossing water, returning herders, tillers and cultivators, mountain sowers, and fishermen.

Pictures of summer should be painted with figures that are peaceful and at ease in mountain groves, in sunlit and shaded places; or travelers resting in water side pavilions and rest houses and avoiding the heat of summer by getting the cool breezes. Depict figures playing in water and floating boats; washing near a river; fetching water from a well at dawn; wading through water or crossing on a ferry in wind and rain. [43]

Pictures of autumn should be painted with mournful looking figures gazing at the moon or figures gathering water chestnuts, washing thin silk, fishermen playing their flutes, figures threshing dark rice, ascending heights [for observance of the 9th day of the 9th moon celebration, when dogwood was carried to high places to ward off misfortune and assure longevity], admiring chrysanthemums, and the like.

Pictures of winter should be painted with figures quietly gathered around a stove, drinking wine in the grievous cold; traveling officials with snow-covered bamboo hats; cold-looking figures in mule-drawn carts;[44] people transporting grain on snowy river fords; figures hunting in the snow of wintry wilds and treading on ice.

In pictures of waters and open fields, you should combine them with birds. Spring pictures should be painted with mountain finches and yellow orioles; summer pictures with seagulls and herons; autumn pictures with migratory geese and flocks of ducks; winter pictures should be painted with scattered wild geese and cawing crows.

Now, I have offered merely generalities in each of the preceding examples, but if you know these thoroughly then you can compose a scene in accordance with its proper season and with allowance for your ability and ideas. Then the ornamental details[45] of your landscape painting will be perfect.

Concerning Defects in the Use of

Brush and Ink, Standards, and Ch'i-yün

Painting is "brush" [drawing], but it is at the same time
an action of the mind/heart. That is to say, even before you begin
to represent forms, you must search into [your heart for them];
but once obtained [you are ready to] represent them in accordance
with painting methods. Painting is in agreement with the
creative forces and has the same origin as the Tao (the root
of all things). Grasping the brush you delve into a myriad images;
wielding the brush you are able to produce scenery of a thousand li.
It is by means of "brush" that one creates form and substance,
and through "ink" that one differentiates light and shade. Hence,
a landscape painting fully depends on "brush" and "ink."

As far as "brush" was concerned, Wu Tao-tzu excelled in
"substance" (chih 質), which is why the substance of his painting
was excellent. [46] It was once said that Wu-Tao-tzu's landscapes
possessed brush but not ink while Hsiang Jung's 項容 landscapes
possessed ink but not brush. [47] In consequence, neither man obtained
perfection. It was only Ching Hao, who, by taking their respective
strong points and making them his own, attained perfection. For,
[in my opinion], if you rely too much on "ink," you destroy the real
substance of the things and injure the "brush," as well as smudge
[the painting surface].

Where the use of "ink" is excessively feeble, the spirit
becomes timid and weak. Both, excess and insufficiency, are defects.

By all means follow rules and standards, but base your
painting on spontaneous ch'i-yün 氣韻. By doing so you will certainly
attain vitality in the painting. A painting that is successful in this is
a perfect thing, but one that fails is defective. In investigations of
this sort, how can one discuss them with a foolish and vulgar person?

Generally, before you even grasp the brush you must
concentrate your spirit and clarify your thoughts; then, in anticipation,
the image will appear before your very eyes. Hence: "The idea
exists before the brush." [48] Afterwards, if by means of standards
you have pushed your ideas forward [to the finished product], then it
can be said that what has been obtained from the mind corresponds to

that which is from the hand. There are various ways of the use of "brush." The "brush" may be simple and easy, yet completely meaningful; it may be skillful and dense, and exquisitely refined; or one may select a spirited style marked by strokes which are virile and powerful; or a pleasing style in which the brushstrokes are flowing and unbroken. There are all sorts of variations which exist in the use of the brush.

But there are many defects in the practice of painting, the most serious of which is vulgarity. It arises from shallowness and superficiality and conforms to the lowly. If a painter does not know standards and has no technical discipline, yet dashes things off with a spontaneous air or forces an antique blandness and dryness --- even though he does it in a kind of exquisite and delicate way, confused and self-conscious forms will ensue and so he will merely concoct something unnaturally antique. This [vulgarity] is called a defect in using brush and ink, standards, and ch'i-yün.

The ancients said: "There are three defects in the use of the brush. The first is described as being like a board; the second as being like an engraving; and the third as being like a knot. Being like a 'board' means that the wrist is weak and the brush sluggish, so that give and take is completely lost. The forms of objects are flat and are not rounded out and are 'board-like' in effect. The 'engraving' defect connotes a brush style which is too obvious in manner, in which the brushstrokes are stiff and angular, resulting in a false liveliness and sharp corners. Being like a 'knot' means that one is poised to proceed but does not, or fails to break off [the line] when one should, or when it appears as if the fluidity of line describing the forms has been obstructed. "[49]

In addition to the preceding, I should also like to suggest a painting defect which I wish to call "hardness" (ch'iu 遒). That is, when a painter only pays attention to trifling matters and foolishly becomes a stickler for inessentials in his brushwork; when he is completely devoid of versatility, even though his "brush" and "ink" are in movement, they are like dead things, his forms seeming to have been carved --- this is the defect of "hardness."

Generally, in using the brush, the first thing painters must seek is ch'i-yün.[50] Next, they must decide upon stylistic essentials, and afterwards, upon subtleties. If,before completion of the formal aspect,the painter applies clever subtleties, then he will perforce lose the ch'i-yün. If he but strive for ch'i-yün in his painting, then as a matter of course, form-likeness (hsing-ssu 形似) will be present in his work.

Moreover, painters should study well the principles of landscape painting. They should maintain a [sense of] reality (shih 實) in their painting. If the reality is insufficient but there is excessive ostentation/showiness (hua 華), such ostentation should be eliminated.[51] Reality connotes substance or corporeality. Ostentatiousness connotes brilliant ornamentation. Substance/corporeality originates from nature, while ornamentation is a man-made thing. Reality is basic [to a painting] whereas ornamentation is not. Nature is essence/substance, art is application. Hence, how can one neglect what is basic and pursue inessentials or be unmindful of the essence and form an attachment to technique? This is like the case of the painter who has only paid attention to brilliance and seductiveness: the substance (t'i 體) and method (fa 法) are lost. As for the painter who has only paid attention to the soft and delicate: the spirit-vitality (shen-ch'i 神氣) is destroyed. These really are examples of the defect of vulgarity! How can such painters know about the principles of preserving reality and eliminating ostentation?

Furthermore, brushmanship is sometimes coarse, sometimes delicate; sometimes uneven, sometimes even; sometimes heavy and sometimes light. If there is no clear distinction between each of these strokes in the arrangement of far to near things,then it will appear to be spiritually weak and the result will not be a painting.

If the brushwork is too coarse, then this weakens the painting's sense of order. If the brushwork is too delicate, then this terminates its flow of ch'i-yün. Each ts'un 皴 (wrinkle), tien 點 (dot), kou 勾 (hook), and cho 斫 (axe-chop) has meaning and follows rules preserved from the past. If one does not follow the painting rules of the ancients and merely copies an actual mountain without distinguishing near and far, shallowness and depth [by means of these strokes], then this is indeed like an illustration in a geography book. How can such a painter attain standards and ch'i-yün in his work?

Generally, there are eight different patterns (ko 格)[52] in landscape painting. There is the aged and damp stone; the pure and clear water; the precipitously assembled mountain; the freely flowing untrammelled spring; the appearing and disappearing clouds and mist; the winding rustic paths; the pine tree like a dragon or a snake; and the wind and rain hiding in the bamboo.

Concerning Acumen in the Examination of Paintings

Everyone is aware of the fact that jasper (ch'iung-kuei 瓊瑰) and wan-yen 琬琰 are beautiful jades. But if it had not been for Pien [Ho's] 卞和 three presentations, [53] who would have recognized those Mt. Ching (荊山) beauties and considered them beautiful? Everyone knows that the hua-liu 驊騮 and the yao-niao 騕褭 [54] were excellent horses. But if it had not been for Po Lo's 伯樂 [55] one glance, who would have discerned the noble horses of Chi Pei 冀北 and considered them excellent? If you have no judgment for jades, how can you grasp the fame of the ch'iung-kuei and wan-yen; if you have no judgment for horses, how can you tell the value of a hua-liu or yao-niao? As far as judgment is concerned, in jades there was only Pien Ho, in horses only Po Lo. Since their time nobody could match or improve on their judgments. This is the same as in the painting of landscape in this generation. Concealed beneath the facts and realities of nature in landscape painting are references to ancient and modern [stylistic] subtleties; manifest in these forms of heaven and earth is the cultivated and refined artistic instruction of sages and worthies. How could a mean and vulgar person ferret out with ease even the least points of landscape painting? For it is likely than an unfathomable spirit and subtleties difficult to explain would be present in such paintings.

Generally, when examining paintings, the first thing to look for is the aspect of ch'i-yün; next has to be studied the level of standards; that is, the application of the former worthies' standards and rules. If a painting's vitality (sheng-i 生意) is pure and its elements are in agreement with reason/order (li 理), its rules perfect, its standards on a high level, such a painting has doubtless succeeded within its particular limitations; but what about a painting which despite such qualities, confuses the traditional methods? Well, if one were to paint in the style of Li Ch'eng, why mix it with that of Fan K'uan's? Just as in calligraphy one would not mix Yen (Chen-ch'ing's) and Liu (Kung-ch'üan's)[56] methods, nor practice seal script (chuan-shu 篆書) and scribe script (li-shu 隸書) at the same time. Hence the saying: If what is grasped cannot be unified, then there will be discrepancies." True? Yes, it is. By turning to the past and examining the present how can one who is good at looking at paintings make no distinctions! Yet, ancient and modern

landscape styles are painting. He who understands painting methods
will comprehend the vitality of spiritual perfection; but he who
studies writing methods will have [in his painting] the defects of a
geography book illustration. One must not ignore these points.

Painters nowadays tend to study but one school, and there
are many who do not understand the accomplishments of the various
famous traditions. While there are able men of wide acquaintance
with the various traditions, few are they who are deeply conversant
with any one of those masters. As for such artists' works, they are
confused in spirit and thought, mixed up in their models and rules,
and for these reasons, extremely difficult to judge. As for elucidating
the older masters' methods, it is only the gentleman possessing
deep comprehension who can discuss clearly their principles. It is
the man who has investigated the stars thoroughly and then verifies
the [geomantically proper location of] a tomb site. [57] Even though
one's undertakings are many, if there is order to them then there
is no confusion; even though things (in general) are multitudinous,
if there is order/sequence to them, there is no disorder. In each
of these cases there is an indwelling sense of right principle (li 理   ).
As for the right principle of examining paintings: if one has not
mellowed his heart and mind, is not good at distinguishing painting
materials, and is not a connoisseur of depth and breadth, then he will
be unable to attain this right principle. Among paintings there are
those that have purity of substance and are limpid and bland; that are
rustic and simple but possess antique awkwardness; that are light
and refined and tersely beautiful; that are loosely arranged and graceful
and airy; that are wild and full of abandon and endowed with aliveness;
that have lonely distances that are deep and far-reaching; that are
dark and dim but whose ideas are clear; that are realistic but
relaxed and easy-going in manner; that are busy with detail but not
confused; that are densely packed but not muddled. All of these
were the accomplishments of painters of the three periods of
antiquity[58] who advanced to the famed ranks of divine (shen 神   ) and
excellent (miao 妙   ). Each was blessed with right principle.

If a painting on first observation appears quite fathomable
but on careful study reveals marvelous effects and increasing
profundity, such a painting is superior. On the other hand, if there
is a painting which on first observation appears unfathomable and
again does so on second glance, but after exhaustive study proves
eccentric in principle and method, such a painting is inferior.

Painters may be likened to gentlemen scholars.
Manifest in their works is a quality like metal and stone
(strength and durability); revealed in their actions is an accord
with rule; if near to them they appear gentle; if judged/seen from
a distance they appear stern; "they are easy to serve and yet
difficult to please;"[59] hard to approach and easily alienated, "in
movements, countenance and every turn of the body, there is nothing
that is not in agreement with right principle."[60] The decorum of
superiors is like this.

But there are painters who may be likened to petty
men, too. With groundless talk they pander to each other; with
pretended actions they compete with each other; approach them and
they ridicule you; stand aloof from them and they show resentment;
merely by flattering or currying favor they adjust their own views
to others; they work so hard at lying they deceive even themselves.
Because they are always engaging in schemes they do not comply in
the least with right principle. The decorum of inferiors is like this.
One must completely understand these matters. If one understands
just one point but not two, or comprehends up to this point, but not
to that, then he will not be able to judge paintings.

The ancients said: "In painting there are six essentials.
The first is called 'spirit' (ch'i 氣). Spirit means to move the brush
in accordance with form and to seize the image without hesitation.
The second is called 'harmony' (yün 韻). Harmony means to conceal
the traces of one's efforts in establishing form so that appearance
will not be commonplace. The third is called 'thought' (ssu 思). Thought
means to suddenly grasp the essentials and concentrate on the general
fitness of things. The fourth is called 'scenery' (ching 景). Scenery
means to follow laws of seasonal change and to search out the sublime
to create the rare. The fifth is called 'brush' (pi 筆). Although the brush
is dependent on methods and rules, its movements are flexible.
Brushwork is neither substance nor ornament. Its effects are like
flight or motion. The sixth is called 'ink' (mo 墨). Ink can distinguish
between highness and lowness in objects through dark and light tones.
Thus, one can differentiate shallowness and depth. These tones will
produce an appearance so natural that it will seem not to be done with
a brush."[61] If a painting is endowed with these six laws, it is a marvel
of the divine (shen 神) class. But even if a painting has not fully
realized these six laws, if it but excel in just one of them it ought not
to be rejected for examination.

[handwritten annotation: painting can possess truth → and can persist on → is Dr. Holland book.]

If a painting has truth, it may be transmitted to posterity.
For a painting whose fame is not self-evident, there is the saying:
"where there is substance, fame will come of itself." Even if such
revelation is not anticipated, the painting will, of its own accord,
become famous. However, even if a painting has a good reputation
at one time, it may gradually diminish in fame in the end. As the
saying goes, if anything is more famous than its actual worth, then
even if its diminution in fame is not anticipated, its reputation will
diminish of its own accord.

Generally, in the appreciation of paintings, how can one
choose on the basis of some official's praise! Merely by looking at
a painting one can consider it excellent if its style is pure and it
has antique ideas; if its ink is marvelous and its brushwork subtle;
if its scenery is quiet and secluded; if its ideas are far-reaching and
its principles profound, and if its manner is lofty in thought.
Paintings not equal to such fineness can be dismissed as mere skilled
and detailed works and are rarely examined.

Among men of this generation there was Wang Chin-ch'ing
王晉卿 (Wang Shen 王詵)[62] who was a cultivated gentleman of the
imperial family. He was well versed in literature and history;
he let his thoughts roam in maps and documents [books]. During
leisure time he would amuse himself with painting small pictures,
many of which he would distribute among the families of the high
ranking officials and nobles. I fortunately received his favor and each
time there was a viewing of paintings, he would summon me to
look at them together with him; he would discuss the subtleties of
the paintings and talk about their fame and authenticity. Unexpectedly
one day at the Tz'u Shu Hall,[63] a Li Ch'eng was hanging on the east
wall and a Fan K'uan on the west. Wang first looked at the Li Ch'eng
and said: "Li Ch'eng's painting method was that of moist ink and fine
brushwork; he depicts mists that lightly move, scenery of a thousand
li that seems to be right before one's eyes; he possesses a fresh
spirit which one can almost grasp." Next he looked at Fan K'uan's
painting and said: "It is just as if the densely packed mountain ranges
were truly lined up before one's eyes; the spirit is strong and
unfettered, and its brushwork is extremely vigorous. As for the
effects of these two paintings --- truly, one is like a civil [thing] and
the other is like a military [thing]." It seems to me that the
appropriateness of his words truly can be called criticism that
penetrates to the very marrow. It is essential to know the main points

of standards and methods.   Then you will be able to distinguish
between what is inferior and superior, what is right and wrong.
Then it can be said that you are a true connoisseur!   If a person
is unable to judge paintings then he is just like the traveler on the
road who cannot distinguish between good and evil --- is it not sad!

        Nowadays there exist paintings by famous high ranking scholar-
officials.   [64]   Making it their leisure time hobby of relaxation and
enjoyment they grasp the brush and wet the tip and by wielding
the brush try to realize their ideas;   many rely on a simple method
in order to obtain a pure and untrammelled taste, a quality which
flows from natural purity and has not one iota of vulgarity.   But
if one takes the present generation's concept of ancient standards,
they cannot be recognized.   However, all of the famous gentlemen
painters of antiquity adhered to standards.   Indeed, since the
Southern T'ang period, in the case of painters such as Li Ch'eng,
Kuo Hsi, Fan K'uan, Yen Kung-mu [Su, also Mu-chih], Sung
Fu-ku [Ti], Li Po-shih [Kung-lin], Wang Chin-ch'ing, and the like ---
it is indeed true that they were knowledgeable about all these
standards. [65]

Concerning Ancient and Modern Scholars

What Heaven has bestowed upon me is my nature. Whereby
my nature will be enriched from other men is learning (or study).
In human nature there are differences between those that are
stupid and those that are intelligent. In studying there are
unlimited benefits through daily acquisition. Thus, we may, in
accordance with the intelligence given by nature, seek this
enrichment through study. There never has been a case of a person
who did not gain from instruction. Moreover, the ancients developed
their own natures by working hard at scholarship, whereas modern
men give insult to scholarship by relying on their natural dispositions.[66]
Therefore, the farther these men are detached from antiquity the
less refined will be their work.

Formerly, when in the summer months Ku K'ai-chih[67]
ascended to the upper level of his tower (studio) his family rarely
saw him. When it was windy, rainy or dark, or when he was
hungry or cold, joyful or angry, he did not take up the brush. In the
T'ang dynasty, Tu Fu dedicated to Wang Wei a poem which read:
"In ten days he painted one stream, in five days he painted one stone ---
the able man will not tolerate pressure."[68] Hardly any genuine works
by Ku K'ai-chih and Wang Wei are left to posterity; what later
imitators were able to achieve were decidedly quite common works.
This is just like the discussion of Tu Fu in the T'ang History:
"The scent of left-over fat lingers on to moisten (i. e. "to bestow its
benefits on") later generations." The ancients used these [paintings]
in order to nourish their spirits during their leisure time, while
men of modern times use them as objects for gain and strenuously
exert themselves towards that end. As Confucius said: "Study, in
antiquity, was for the sake of self-improvement, whereas in modern
times it is done for the sake of impressing others."[69] Formerly,
men of taste, both in and out of office, considered it their favorite,
personal pleasure during their leisure time in quiet, secluded places.
Chang Yen-yüan of the T'ang dynasty said that the art of painting and
calligraphy cannot be learned by the children of villagers.[70] But what
about present-day scholars who frequently take painting to be a lofty
trade, considering their pictures as a means for profit? Having lost
the inspiration for learning (literally: "the inspiration of the nine
schools") and failing to cultivate the scholar-artist's attitude, are
they not making light of their art? Their lack of refinement may well
originate here. Abandoning, as the saying goes, the roots/essentials,
they pursue non-essentials.

Those men who are without learning may be said to be without standards --- that is, without the standards and methods of the ancients. How can such men discard standards and methods and consider themselves superior to the renowned ancient and modern sages? A gentleman said to be of scant learning is one whose nature is excessively impetuous. There are three types of such self-deceivers. As for those who have difficulties in learning there are two types. What is meant by this? Of the three types --- there is one who is so ambitious that he unashamedly seeks knowledge from inferiors and relies merely on pilfered knowledge --- he is self-deceiving. Then there is one who is, by nature, clever, and whose talents are great, but who haphazardly studies, is confused and without a definite purpose --- he is self-deceiving. Then there is one who, during his youth, was precocious and effortlessly became rather well versed, but who is lazy and does not study --- he is self-deceiving.

But what about the difficult learners? There is the blind scholar who does not understand the principles of scholarship, who carelessly trusts to luck. Then there is the scholar who pretends to study with laborious efforts but who exerts his energies in a purpose which is obscure and confused, without even investigating into truth. Such types are really inferior.

How does one transmit the relics ("dregs") of the ancients or arrive at the secrets of former sages? "No one has ever become skilled by not studying." How true are these words! Generally, a scholar should first adhere to one school's fixed methods. Then, after he has successfully mastered them, he may change them to create his own style. Ah! If one's roots are deep, his reputation will be long. One who manifests propriety will reflect correctness. Accordingly, it is study that leads to the creation of the "marvelous," and to the perfection of purity in art. Those who possess these roots are indeed like this.

Notes

1. The *Preface* sets the high moral tone for the text. While obligatory and heavily dependent on past writers, particularly Chang Yen-yüan, it nonetheless leaves no doubt about the author's predilection for landscape painting.

2. Fu Hsi: a legendary emperor said to have had the body of a snake and the head of a man. Chang Yen-yüan is *Li-tai ming-hua chi* (hereafter referred to as LTMHC), Chapter I, Sect. I, says: "When P'ao Hsi [another name for Fu Hsi], made his discovery [a reference to the Dragon-horse with the trigrams on his back] at the shining (Yellow) River, this was the germ of all tablets and books, charts and paintings." See Wm. R. B. Acker translation in *Some T'ang and Pre-T'ang Texts on Chinese Painting* (hereafter referred to as *Some T'ang*), Leiden, 1954, p. 62. Fu Hsi was thought to be a literary and artistic primogenitor which explains his high ranking in both these texts. Further information on Fu Hsi is to be found in *ibid.*, pp. 87-89.

3. Shih Huang and Ts'ang Chieh are legendary figures difficult to identify as they are sometimes considered as one person. However, in the present context, they seem to be separated. Acker gives information on them but does not come to any definite conclusion although he considers them as two figures. *Ibid.*, p. 93f.

4. Han Cho is paraphrasing Chang Yen-yüan; see Acker, *op. cit.*, Chapter I, Sect. I, p. 62f.

5. Quoted from Ching Hao: *Pi-fa chi.* See Shio Sakanishi translation in *The Spirit of the Brush* (hereafter referred to as *Spirit*), London, 1948, p. 87, "Painting is delimitation." The entire paragraph containing the Ching Hao quotation is a paraphrase of a passage in the *Preface* of *T'ang-ch'ao ming-hua lu* (herafter referred to as TCMHL) by Chu Ching-hsüan. See A. Soper tr. in *Archives of the Chinese Art Society of America*, IV, 1950, p. 8.

6. This is quoted from Kuo Jo-hsü, T'u-hua chien-wen chih (hereafter referred to as THCWC), ch. 5. See Soper translation in Kuo Jo-hsü's Experiences in Painting (hereafter referred to as Experiences), p. 79. "In this life I tarry among nonsensical words; In my former body I must have been a master-painter, ..." The quotation is also to be found in the earlier TCMHL. See Soper tr., Archives, p. 14.

7. Although Han Cho mentions ten chapters there is general agreement that one of these chapters is missing in the text as it now stands. The Shuo-fu edition and the MSTS, IV edition have a "Chapter Ten" titled "Lun san ku chih hua kuo yü pu chi" (論三古之書過與不及), but its inclusion as part of the original text is disputed. The chapter, as Aoki observes, is of slight interest and adds little to the preceding chapters. Another opinion is expressed by Yü Shao-sung in Shu-hua shu-lu chieh-t'i: "My opinion is that [the section called] "Scenery of the Four Seasons" in Chapter 6 was [originally] considered as a separate chapter since the sentences are unconnected [with what precedes] and there is also no connection with the subject of figure painting, etc.; hence, it was later men who mistakenly made the connection [between the two parts] and transmitted the document thus to this time." The preceding is quoted in Ssu-pu tsung-lu, op. cit., p. 723b. This seems an interesting and convincing argument.

8. There are two dates given in the MSTS versions. MSTS, IV, No. 10, has July 23, 1121 (宣和辛丑歲季夏几日). MSTS, II, No. 8, has August 2, 1121 (宣和歲在辛丑季夏月十几日). Aoki follows the former dating and I have adhered to it. In any event, the two dates are not far apart; the latter is probably a misprint.

9. Wang Wei was more specific in his essay Shan-shui lun. See Sakanishi, Spirit, p. 71: "The mountains should be in scores of feet...

10. Ching Hao, Pi-fa chi. Sakanishi, ibid., p. 91.

11. The Wang-shih hua-yüan edition (hereafter referred to as WSHY) has 溪中有水也 which does not seem correct. Aoki has substituted 谷 for 溪 and I follow him here.

12. Cf. Kuo Hsi, Lin-ch'üan kao-chih (hereafter referred to as LCKC), as translated in Sakanishi, An Essay on Landscape Painting (hereafter referred to as Essay), London, 1959, pp. 38-39.

13. The Kuo Hsi quotation, slightly amended (note in particular, the phrase "seeing in the background faintly colored mountains") is from LCKC; cf. Sakanishi, ibid., p. 49. Han Cho, a younger contemporary of Kuo Hsi, emphasizes atmospheric effects in his three additional "distances" --- an indication, perhaps, of Chao Ling-jang's influence on early 12th century landscape ideas. He also speaks of "scenery which is incomplete," a foretaste, perhaps, of Ma Yüan - Hsia Kuei compositions.

14. Sakanishi, Essay, p. 48. Cf. Kuo Hsi's analogy of a mountain with the human physiognomy.

15. In this paragraph I have followed Aoki and MSTS, IV, 10.

16. From Mencius, Bk. IV, Pt. II, Ch. 18/2; see Legge, The Chinese Classics, reprint, Hong Kong, 1960, Vol. II, p. 324.

17. The closest source that I have been able to find for this quotation is in Wang Wei's Hua-hsüeh pi-chüeh. It reads: 莫作連綿之道 ("Do not make continuous roads.")

18. Han Cho is paraphrasing Ching Hao. See Sakanishi, Spirit, p. 89.

19. Aoki follows the Shuo-fu edition which has 翬 instead of 脉 in the WSHY. I have followed Aoki and the Shuo-fu.

20. I am following the MSTS, IV, 10 version.

21. The dramatic postures of the pine trees described in this passage are at variance with the more noble and stately pines of which Ching Hao writes in Pi-fa chi: "To paint them as soaring or coiling dragons with their branches and needles in mad confusion, therefore, is not at all in harmony with the spirit and rhythm of the pines." Sakanishi, Spirit, p. 90. One must remember that Ching Hao's old rustic is making a distinction between idealized pines and real ones --- "that outward forms should never be taken for inner realities." Han Cho is closer to Kuo Jo-hsü; see Soper, Experiences, p. 11: "In doing woods or single trees, there will be drooping branches and upstanding trunks, crooked joints and furrowed bark; their bonds splitting apart into a multitude of [twig] tips, and subdividing into a myriad forms. One will create the effect of furious dragons or fearful serpents, or build up an atmosphere of chill clouds and an overcast sun. It will be proper to make them cliff-like in their luxuriant loftiness, and to give an ancient sturdiness to their coiling roots." Unlike both these writers, Han Cho

seems more concerned with specific ways of painting trees in the rest of this chapter. In this, he is more "realistic" than Ching Hao and even Kuo Jo-hsü. Also, in his preference for the picturesque he seems to forecast the trees of Southern Sung landscapes.

21a. This is a quotation from the <u>Lun-yü</u>, II, 14. Legge, <u>op. cit.</u>, Vol. I, p. 150.

22. Han Cho transcribed incorrectly the line from Ching Hao's <u>Pi-fa chi</u>. The <u>Hua-lun ts'ung-k'an</u> edition of the Ching Hao text reads: 成林者 爽氣重榮，不能者抱節自屈　. The character <u>ts'ai</u> 材 was probably mistranscribed for <u>lin</u> 林. With this one character rectified, Han Cho's meaning comes close to the original.

23. This quotation does not appear in Wang Wei's text. However, it does appear in Liang Yüan Ti's text, <u>Shan-shui sung shih ko</u> ("On the categories of landscapes, pines, and rocks"), MSTS, III, 9. See note 25 below. Han Cho has <u>li</u> 離 for <u>nan</u> 難, which latter gives better sense. Possibly, the present version of the Yüan Ti text is corrupt.

24. This too, does not appear in Wang Wei's text. Aoki follows the <u>Shuo-f</u> edition. He substitutes 不 for 下. I believe the original is correct.

24a. In contrast, the ancient lexical works, the <u>Erh ya</u> (c. 3rd cent. B.C.) and <u>Shuo wen</u> (c. A.D. 100), liken the leaves of the cypress, not the bark, to a cedar.

25. Yüan Ti of the Liang dynasty, also known as Hsiao I 蕭繹 (506-554), was a renowned scholar and figure painter. The text which Han Cho quotes is the <u>Shan-shui sung shih ko</u> of note 23. This is a brief and problematic text, undoubtedly much later in date than its alleged author. It may be early Sung in origin as that is the period when it first appears (in the compilation <u>Sung i-wen-chih</u> 宋藝文志). Han Cho must have been familiar with the text as he quotes it correctly. He is at his most didactic, however, in explaining what seems obvious. See Sakanishi, <u>Spirit</u>, Chapter V, for translation.

26. These passages do not appear in Yüan Ti's text.

27. I am following Aoki and the <u>Shuo-fu</u> edition. The sentence begins 遠木者取其大要　.

28. This does not appear in Yüan Ti's text.

29. This paragraph has been discussed by Soper in "Some Technical Term in the Early Literature of Chinese Painting," <u>Harvard Journal of Asiatic Studies</u>, 1948, v. 11, p. 169. <u>Cf.</u> his "The fall of the ink [must bring out] solidity and hardness. Concavities will be deep, convexities shallow; 'wrinkle-dabbing' [will establish] the shaded and

sunlit [surfaces]." (落墨聖寶凹深凸淺皴拂陰陽). See
also Soper, Experiences, p. 11, and note 126.

30. Goepper, Essence of..., p. 67, translates p'i-ma ts'un as "scattered
hemp fibers." He writes: "So far as I know this is the first document
[Han Cho's text] that mentions this fundamental form of the various
ts'un with which the interior drawing of rounded mountain summits
is rendered by relatively long, curving brush lines. It provides the
starting point for the various other types and is probably the oldest
in the mature landscape painting; in any case, it already appears in
pictures which are attributed to the fathers of landscape painting
in the tenth century or at least embody their style."

31. There seems to be no specific source for this, although Kuo Hsi may
have inspired Han Cho: "A mountain viewed at a close range has one
appearance; a mountain viewed at a distance of several miles has
another." Sakanishi, Essay, p. 40. What Han Cho seems to be
putting in the mouths of the ancients may actually be his own idea. Yet,
the quotation and the paragraph in which it appears seem enigmatic
(and are perhaps corrupt). However, the whole indicates his interest
in the essential appearance of things. Aoki points out that Huang
Kung-wang (of the Yüan) in Hsieh shan-shui chüeh gives a partial
quotation of the line.

32. Yü-i refers to Yang-ku 暘谷 ("Valley of the sun"), the land in the east
which during the legendary Emperor Yao's time was considered the
easternmost part of the empire; reputed to be a place in Korea.

33. Aoki proposes 雲色 for 雪色 in the WSHY edition. I am following
his interpretation.

34. MSTS, IV, 10, has 大概以雲別. The WSHY has 形 for 別.
I am following the former.

35. The Erh ya: 3rd century B. C. dictionary of terms and phrases.

36. Aoki points out that Han Cho is misquoting the Erh ya. The
Erh ya version has: 風而雨土. Han Cho's: 風而雨之.

37. Han Cho embellishes here. The Erh ya reads: 陰而風為曀
whereas Han Cho has: 陰風重而為曀.

38. Aoki follows the Shuo-fu edition. The WSHY edition reads: 此皆
不時之氣也霏雪之流. The Shuo-fu has: 此皆不時之氣非
雲之所議也. I have followed the latter in my translation.

39. Lü-shih ch'un-ch'iu, ch. 13. 山雲草莽，水雲魚鱗，旱雲煙火，雨雲水波，無不皆類，其所生以示人，故以龍致雨，以形逐影．("Mountain clouds [like] grassy vegetation, water clouds like fish scales, drought clouds like smoky fires, rain clouds like water ripples. They all resemble that which has brought them forth, so as to make it visible to men. Thus, it is the dragon who causes rain and a form that is followed by its shadow.") Cf. R. Wilhelm, Frühling und Herbst des Lü Bu We, Jena, 1928, p. 161.

40. Lu Chi (261-303), styled Shih-heng 士衡． An eminent writer of the Chin dynasty (265-316). The poem referred to is "Fu-yün fu" (浮雲賦)．

41. I am following the Shuo-fu edition here.

42. The P'ei-wen-chai and Hua-lun ts'ung-k'an editions have 或旋以． MSTS, IV, 10, has 或拖以． I have followed the latter.

43. I have followed MSTS, IV, 10, for this passage. It reads: 濯水浮舟臨江浴滌曉汲涉水風雨過渡之類也 ． This seems preferable to the HLTK edition which goes: 濯水浮梁．浴鶴江游曉汲涉水過渡之類也 ．

44. The character 軿 is perhaps mistranscirbed for yu 輶 (also written 輶) meaning "light carriage" or "cart."

45. Professor Max Loehr has suggested that the term chuang-shih 裝飾 corresponds to the French term staffage as used in art-historical terminology. I have followed his suggestion.

46. This is patterned on what Ching Hao in Pi-fa chi said: 吳道子筆勝於象骨氣自高樹不言圖亦恨無墨 ． Sakanishi translates: "As to Wu Tao-tzu, his brushwork excelled his representation; his work has such a high tone that no one can say anything against it. It is a pity, however, that he lacked ink." Spirit, p. 94. For Ching Hao's hsiang 象 ("representation"), Han Cho substitutes chih 質, which implies "basic foundation" or "substance;" apparently "representation" was no longer a live issue in discussing Wu Tao-tzu's work.

47. Again, Han Cho is borrowing from Ching Hao. This passage can also be found in Kuo Jo-hsü's THCWC. See Experiences, p. 26, under Ching Hao.

48. The earliest instance of this idea appears in a text on calligraphy, the "Colophon" to <u>Pi Chen T'u</u>, traditionally attributed to Wang Hsi-chih (321-379) but probably around A. D. 618. "Let the concept precede the brush --- only then does one write." See Richard M. Barnhart, "Wei Fu-jen's <u>Pi Chen T'u</u> and the Early Texts on Calligraphy," <u>Archives of the Chinese Art Society</u>, Vol. XVIII, 1964, p. 21. Also to be found in Wang Wei's treatise titled "Shan-shui lun," first line. Also quoted by Chang Yen-yüan, LTMHC, <u>inter alia</u>, and by Kuo Jo-hsü, THCWC, section titled "On virtues and faults in brushwork," <u>Experiences</u>, p. 16.

49. This passage is taken from Kuo Jo-hsü, THCWC, <u>Experiences</u>, <u>ibid</u>.

50. This refers to the famous first law or canon of painting as enunciated by Hsieh Ho (c. 6th c.) in <u>Ku hua-p'in lu</u>. See Acker, <u>Some T'ang</u>, p. 4 and Sakanishi, <u>Spirit</u>, p. 50. Han Cho is using it as a basic condition for good painting, not dependent upon technique yet somehow related to the ability to reproduce "form-likeness" (<u>hsing-ssu</u>).

51. The <u>Shuo-fu</u> edition has 當去其華 . The WSHY edition reads: 當棄其筆 . I am following the former and Aoki, p. 124.

52. <u>Ko</u> (格) has hitherto been translated as "standards" but in this paragraph the meaning seems to be more limited and specific in scope. Hence, I have translated it as "patterns."

53. An 8th century B. C. man of Ch'u whose story is recorded by Han Fei-tzu. In his selfless recommendation of the Mt. Ching jade he suffered the loss of both feet due to the skepticism of two sovereigns to whom he presented the stone. In the end, his faith prevailed when a third prince recognized its true worth. See Giles, <u>Biographical Dictionary</u> (hereafter referred to as B. D.), No. 1650.

54. The character 驣 seems to be a variant of 裊 (niao, also written 裊 , 嬝). Combined with 驊, it refers to an excellent horse of antiquity (see Morohashi, <u>Dai Kanwa Jiten</u>, 12/44841).

55. The sobriquet of a famous horse-trainer, named Sun Yang, who lived in remote antiquity and is mentioned by Chuang-tze. Giles, B. D. , 1661.

56. Two famous calligraphers of the T'ang dynasty. Yen Chen-ch'ing (A. D. 709-785). Giles, B. D. , 2461; Liu Kung-ch'üan (A. D. 778-865). B. D. 1325.

57. Goepper, Essence of..., pp. 147-148, discusses geomancy and landscape painting.

58. I.e., High Antiquity: Chin-Sung 晋宋, Middle Antiquity: T'ang 唐 , Recent Antiquity: Five Dynasties 五代 .

59. This is a quotation from the Lun-yü, Bk. 13, Chapter XXV: 君子易事而難說 . "The superior man is easy to serve and difficult to please." Legge, The Chinese Classics, Vol. I, p. 273.

60. This is a quotation from Mencius, Part II, Chapter XXXIII: 動容周旋中禮者,盛德之至也 . "When all the movements, in the countenance and every turn of the body, are exactly what is proper, that shows the extreme degree of the complete virtue." Legge, ibid., Vol. II, p. 495.

61. The six essentials which Han Cho discusses are taken from Ching Hao's Pi-fa chi. Ching Hao's six essentials correspond in some respects to Hsieh Ho's six laws. See Spirit, p. 83-84, 87.

62. Wang Shen 王詵. Born c. 1046, died after 1100. From T'ai-yüan, Shansi. Active in second half of the 11th century. Son-in-law of Emperor Ying-tsung; friend of Su Shih (1036-1101). Connoisseur and collector. Landscapes after Li Ssu-hsün (651-716) and Li Ch'eng (919-967). In Han Cho's account of Wang Shen's connoisseurship, it should be remembered that he was Han Cho's patron.

63. Tz'u-shu T'ang 賜書堂 ("Hall of Conferred Books"). The name of a library owned by Sung Shou 宋綬 (991-1040) of the Sung dynasty. From P'ing-chi 平棘 . Tzu: Kung-ch'ui 公垂 . Posthumous title was Hsüan-hsien 宣獻 . He was well versed in history and classics, and possessed an extensive collection of books. A government official.

64. In this concluding paragraph I am following the Shuo-fu edition. Aoki, op. cit., p. 132, notes 1 and 2, comments that the 54 characters following 士大夫 in the WSHY are corrupt. Furthermore the passage which immediately follows in the same edition is an extract from the Hsüan-ho hua-p'u, Preface dated 1120, and concerns Ching Hao. Aoki believes this is an insertion by a later writer and has nothing to do with the contents of the Han Cho chapter. The Shuo-fu edition leaves out this portion and concludes with what seems to be a more appropriate ending. I have followed this in my translation.

65. It is interesting to note that of all the painters mentioned, Kuo Hsi is the sole Painting Academician. J. Cahill observed in <u>Wu Chen,</u> U. of Michigan PhD thesis, 1961, p. 73, n. 67: "Wang [Shen] and Li [Kung-lin] are the only two painters close to his own time whom Han Cho includes in his list of scholar-painters who had "adhered" to the rules."

66. This recalls what Kuo Hsi said in LCKC. See <u>Essay</u>, p. 54: "Men of today, however, are swept away by their impulses and feelings, and rush to complete their work."

67. Although Han Cho relates the following as an anecdote about Ku K'ai-chih, the original story is about a painter named Ku Chün-chih 顧駿之　 and was first recounted by Hsieh Ho in KHPL, Section titled "The Second Class" (第二品). See Acker, <u>Some T'ang</u>, pp. 11-12. Chang Yen-yüan repeats the story in LTMHC, Chapter I, Section IV. <u>Ibid.</u>, pp. 152-153. Quite probably, Han Cho was following Kuo Hsi's error in attributing the story to Ku K'ai-chih. See Kuo Hsi, <u>Hua i,</u> Sakanishi, <u>Essay</u>, p. 52.

68. As in the case mentioned in the preceding note, Han Cho mis-quotes the original. The Tu Fu poem is: "Poem playfully written on the landscape painting of the painter Wang Tsai" (戲題王宰畫山水 圖歌). See von Zach, <u>Tu Fu's Gedichte</u>, VII, 31, for a German translation. As the title indicates, the painting was by Wang Tsai, a painter of the T'ang dynasty and not Wang Wei. See <u>T'ang Sung hua-chia jen ming tz'u-tien,</u> pp. 16-17 for Wang Tsai's biography and mention of the poem. The peom is also referred to by Chu Ching-hsüan in TCMHL, though in slightly changed form: "For ten days he painted one pine, for five days he painted one stone." MSTS, II, 6, section "Miao-p'in shang" (妙品上). Kuo Hsi also quoted it in LCKC. See Sakanishi, <u>Essay</u>, p. 63. Huang T'ing-chien (A.D. 1045-1105) used it as inspiration for a poem titled "On Kuo Hsi's Painting of the Autumn Mountains," translated by Wm. A. Roulston in <u>Oriental Art</u>, 1965, Vol. XI, No. 2, p. 94. "Withal he dared to work leisurely and with meticulous care. He took five days or ten days to paint a stream or a rock."

69. Lun-yü <u>(The Analects of Confucius)</u>, XIV·25 (Ssu-shu tu-pen ed. p. 251). Legge, <u>op. cit.</u>, Vol. I, p. 285.

70. This is from LTMHC, the last paragraph of Section IV, Chapter I. See Acker, <u>Some T'ang</u>, p. 153.

Part II

Hua-chi

Chapters Nine and Ten

By Teng Ch'un

<u>Hua-chi</u>, Chapter Nine:

Concerning the Distant Past

Painting is the acme of culture. Hence, ancient and
modern men in great number have written their opinions on it.
A majority of the successive generations of painters whom
Chang Yen-yüan[1] enumerated were officials. In the T'ang dynasty
Shao-ling's 少陵 [2] poems were minutely and exhaustively descriptive,[3]
and Ch'ang-li's 昌黎 [4] written account[5] did not neglect the slightest
trifle. As for our dynasty there were Wen-chung Ou kung 文忠歐公 , [6]
the three Su 蘇 ,[7] father and sons, the two Ch'ao brothers, [8] Shan-ku
山谷 ,[9] Hou-shan 後山 , [10] Wan-ch'iu 宛邱 ,[11] Huai-hai 淮海 , [12]
Yüeh-yen 月巖 , [13] Man-shih 漫仕 , [14] and Lung-mien 龍眠 . [15]
They commented upon and classified works of art with purity and
loftiness or they wielded the brush in an extraordinary and outstanding
way. But as for painting, how can it be said to be the only art?
My opponents think that since antiquity there have been literary men,
besides those several I have mentioned, who had no ability and
furthermore, no love for painting. I would answer them: "Those
who are well versed in literature but do not understand painting are
few; those who are not versed in literature and yet understand
painting are few. "

The uses of painting are truly vast. The things that make
up the world are myriad. As for all of those things, the painter,
by licking his brush and revolving his thoughts, can exhaustively
portray their characteristics, but there is only one method by which
he can do this. What is that? It is called "transmitting their soul. "
People commonly believe that only human beings have souls; they
do not realize that everything has a soul. Hence, [Kuo] Jo-hsü deeply
despised the work of artisans of which he said that though it was called
"painting" it was not; he said they were able to transmit only their
forms and not their soul. Therefore, he considered <u>ch'i-yün sheng-tung</u>
of the [six] painting laws to be supreme and had trust only in high
officials and [recluses of] cliffs and caves. [16] He was right, of course!

From former times, critics divided painters into three categories: "divine" (shen 神), "excellent" (miao 妙), and "able" (neng 能). It was only Chu Ching-chen of the T'ang dynasty who wrote T'ang-hsien hua-lu ("Catalogue of Worthy Painters of the T'ang Dynasty"),[17] who added another to these three categories: 逸 i ("untrammelled"). After him, Huang Hsiu-fu wrote I-chou ming-hua-chi ("Famous Painters of I-chou")[18] and placed the i category first, before the divine, excellent and able categories. Still, Chu Ching-chen said: "The i category is not restrained by orthodox laws; its use is to show [the painters'] complete range in quality."[19] Considering its being regarded so highly, why should it be placed after the other three categories? Was Hsiu-fu not correct in promoting it to the top position? Finally, since Emperor Hui-tsung specifically esteemed the painting categories the order has been shen, i, miao, and neng.

I have, for some time past, taken up the literary works of famous officials of the T'ang and Sung --- every painting account and poem about painting --- and studied them exhaustively. Thus, I have been able to understand a little from their criticism. Only Huang Shan-ku 黄山谷 (T'ing-chien) was most pure and severe. Yüan-chang 元章 (Mi Fei) had a lofty mind and an excellent eye, but there were occasions when he overstepped the bounds of propriety in his arguments. As for the two venerable scholars, Shao-ling and Tung-p'o, even though they did not exclusively devote themselves to painting, their characters were of such inherent loftiness that against expectation they would just naturally find the right word. Tu Fu said: "their extraordinary [beauty] moves the palace walls;"[20] to convey [the beauty of] the figures painted on the wall, he had to use the word tung 動 to be able to completely express it. He also said: "Please sir, release your brush and make a straight trunk,"[21] in regard to the occasion of using the brush to create the beauty of a very tall pine; without the word fang 放 he would have been unable to transmit this idea. Finally, Su Tung-p'o also went into great detail about painting principles. For example, in lines such as "One who knows truth from the beginning banishes the roots of pettiness; his knowledge is not to be compared with the licentious and dissipated profligate's superficial wisdom."[22a] And "When my brush touches paper, it goes as fast as the wind and rain; before my brush has finished, my spirit has swallowed up all before it."[22b] Was it not the former Ku K'ai-chih and Lu T'an-wei[23] who were able to guide us in these words?

While writing this record, I only set forth elevated and
refined painters of two groups (high officials and recluses of cliffs
and caves);[24] other groups I did not seriously draw up for criticism.
One who sees [a painting] can then hand down words [of judgment];
as for one who only hears about it, how can he lightly criticize it?
I have examined Kuo Jo-hsü's discussion of the T'ien Yü 天玉
("Celestial Jade") pictures by Sun Wei 孫位 [25] and Ching P'o 景朴 26
on the Ying T'ien temple gate at Ch'eng-tu. He says: "The two
works of art contended for supremacy. They were that period's
popular spectacles. The entire city --- gentry and commoners ---
who saw them, overflowed [the temple]."[27] I once examined the
pictures, studying them carefully from below. Then I knew that
P'o had striven for the strange and unusual by imitating Wei, just
as Tu Mo's 杜默 [28] poetry was in imitation of Lu T'ung 盧同 29 and
Ma I 馬異.[30] Kuo Jo-hsü had not once entered Shu (Szechwan).
Merely relying on what he heard, he vainly hoped to compare them.
Was this because of Ou-yang Chiung's 歐陽炯 mistake?[31] Yet he
may have an excuse because he makes additional reference to Hsin
Hsien's 辛顯 discussion[32] which says that P'o's painting was very
far from equalling Wei's. He also regards this commentary as
doubtful. This is why I have drawn up so few for criticism.

There are often omissions in what Kuo Jo-hsü has recorded,
such as "Flowers and Birds" done by Wang Ning 王凝[33] of Chiang-nan
Province; "Great Lake Rocks" by a monk of Jun-chou named Hsiu-fan
修範;[34] the Taoist Liu Chen-po's 劉貞白 [35] "Pines, Rocks, Plums,
and Sparrows;" "Figures, Fairies, and Buddha" by natives of Shu named
T'ung Hsiang 童祥 [36] and Hsü Chung-cheng 許中正 ;[37] Ch'iu
Jen-ch'ing's 丘仁慶 [38] "Flowers" and Wang Yen-ssu's 王延嗣 39
"Demons." All of these were celebrated pictures. All were active
before the Hsi-ning era (1067-1077).

There are many commonplace snow scenes by landscapists.
However, once I saw Ying-ch'iu's 營邱 (Li Ch'eng) "Snow" picture.
Its mountain peaks, forests and buildings were painted in pale ink
and in the empty spaces of water and sky, he filled up with chalky powder.
It was altogether wonderful. Whenever I tell other painters about
this work, without being startled or surprised they merely smile and
laugh: which is enough to show how mediocre and inferior present-day
painters are.

Li Ch'eng was a person of great genius and satisfactory learning. When he was young he had great ambitions --- he often took but never passed his examinations; in the end, since he was unsuccessful he set forth his ideas in painting. As for the wintry forests he composed, many are among cliffs and caves, cut off from inferiors and completely free; they allude to gentlemen out of office. As for the remaining trees, their entire lives are [passed] on the level ground; they allude to petty men who hold [official] positions. His (Li Ch'eng's) ideas were subtle. The Lung-t'u 龍圖 [40] official, Chi Meng 李蒙 said: "During the airings of books of the Hsüan-ho Imperial Treasury I have often observed that there were only very few of Li Ch'eng's large and small landscapes. Nowadays, in officials' and commoners' houses there are landscapes which each family has self-styled as a 'Li Ch'eng.' I do not believe it!"[41]

As for the six laws of painting, it is difficult to combine them all. Only Wu Tao-tzu of the T'ang dynasty and Li Po-shih (Li Kung-lin) of the present dynasty were able to combine them. Wu's brush was unrestrained; regardless of long walls or large scrolls it sent forth wonders without cease. Po-shih was extremely stubborn; only on Ch'eng-hsin-t'ang paper[42] did he transmit wonders and display his skill. If no large calligraphy of his has ever been seen, it is not because of his inability but rather because of his extreme pretence: he was afraid it might possibly link him to the doings of the common artisans.

Mi Yüan-chang wrote: "During the three years that Po-shih had an ailing arm, I began to paint."[43] Although it seems that he was yielding to Po-shih,[44] of himself he said that he imitated the noble antiqueness of Ku [K'ai-chih] and did not employ one stroke in the manner of Master Wu [Tao-tzu], and specialized in painting portraits of loyal men and worthy sages of antiquity; for such an inflexible spirit as his could not bear to be placed below Po-shih.

As for the given forms of birds and animals, grasses, and trees --- those which are in the 5 regions [north, south, east, west and center], they all are, of course, different. But those who look at paintings, judging solely on the basis of what they see in their own districts and arguing that the form-likenesses are not identical --- regarding them as either too small or too large, too long or too short, too fat or too thin --- mutually derisive, taking their talk for reality --- they are not good at looking.

Although Shu is an out-of-the-way and distant place it
has more painters than other areas. In Li Fang-shu's 李方叔
record of paintings in the Te-yü-chai 德隅齋 [45] ("Library of
Virtuous Corners"), half of the [listed] painters lived in Shu.
[Chao] Te-lin 趙德麟 [46] was a member of the royal family; he
had a collection of paintings numbering several ten boxes, all of
which he left behind in the capital [when he was sent to Hsiang-yang,
Hupei]. Only those paintings of the most excellent quality in his
Hsiang-yang library were recorded [in Li's catalogue]. There
were many of these. Shu scholars were really thriving!

The i ("untrammelled") category of painting reached its
highest point with Sun Wei. Later painters became more and more
violent and wild. Although Shih K'o 石恪 [47] and Sun T'ai-ku 孫太古 [48]
were generally acceptable, even they did not escape rudeness and
vulgarity. Finally, there were Kuan-hsiu 貫休 [49] and Yün-tzu
雲子 [50] and their class; there was nothing about which they had
scruples. Their aspirations were high but the results were always
inferior. It was actually futile for those men to try.

Although Shu has had many [painters of] Arhats, the most
famous was Lu Leng-chia 盧棱伽, [51] and next to him in fame were
Tu Ts'o 杜措 [52] and Ch'iu Wen-po 丘文播 , [53] senior and junior
respectively. Many of Leng-chia's works were stereotyped compositions,
only seated and standing images. As to guardians' and worshipers'
images, flower, rock, pine, bamboo, bird and animal paintings, as
he painted none there are none to see. Although there are paintings
of this type painted by both Tu and Ch'iu, their ideas were not very
pure or lofty. All were shy of the skill of Wu Tung-ch'ing 武洞清
of Ch'ang-sha. [54]

According to tradition, Yang Hui-chih 楊惠之 [55] and
Wu Tao-tzu both learned under the same master; Wu Tao-tzu was
accomplished in his studies. Yang Hui-chih was afraid of being
compared with Wu Tao-tzu in fame; he turned to the modeling
of images (in clay) --- thus, both men became the first in the world
(in their respective fields). Consequently, in Chung-yüan 中原 [56]
there are many of Yang Hui-chih's landscapes modeled on walls.
Kuo Hsi saw them and drew a new concept from them. Accordingly,
he ordered a plasterer to not use the trowel, but to rub the plaster
on the wall only with the hand. Whether with hollows or projections,

the whole surface was left uneven. After the plaster dried, he used
ink and followed the forms and marks, shading in the mountain peaks,
forests and streams, adding towers and pavilions and human figures,
as if they were heaven-made. They were called "shadow-walls"
(ying-pi 影壁). Afterwards, such compositions were very plentiful.
These were lingering ideas of Sung Fu-ku 宋復古 who stretched
white silk over ruined walls.[57]

     Generally, hoarded old paintings are often not complete.
Even pieces of cut silk or scraps of paper --- all are considered precious
and worthy of care. Moreover, eight or nine of ten of the most
knowledgeable experts and intelligent scholars happen to be ashamed
of checking the completeness of their collections. As a result, the
untrained laymen often view their collections as incomplete and
worthless. How would they know the age of paintings that have
survived till now --- at the most 500 years old, at the least 200 or
300 years? How would they still be complete? As for cut gold
and broken jade, each is precious.

     Jung Chi's 榮輯 son, Yung 邕 ,[58] was extremely fond
of painting and he endeavored to make his collection as broad as
possible. Each year during the san-fu period (the hottest summer
weather) he aired them, taking each according to category. He
spread them out in order, completely filling his house; every day
he changed the category. It took ten days from beginning to end.
Few rich collectors can compare with him [in terms of care and
attention].

     I was told by an old man that "once, during peaceful
times,[59] some unfilial sons mortgaged a box of paintings to someone ---
altogether there were more than ten pictures, each of which was
cut in half, either horizontally or vertically down the middle. Such
was the case with [Wang] Wei's mountain picture, Tai [Sung's] calf
picture, Hsü Hsi's "Hibiscus and Peach Blossom" picture, and
Ts'ui Po's "Bird and Animal" picture; none was complete. The
reason was that the brothers of the family, who were utterly
immoral, had divided all those paintings between themselves,
thinking that if they did not do that then it would not have been fair."
Really, it is very sad and deplorable.

Hua-chi, Chapter Ten:

Concerning the Recent Past

  When Emperor Hui-tsung's "Dragon Virtue Palace"
(Lung Te Kung 龍德宮)was completed, he ordered the tai-chao
("Painters-in-Attendance") to paint the screens and walls of this
palace. They were among the best painters of the time. When the
Emperor came to inspect [their work], he had not a single word of
praise; all he did was look at "Rose of the Month on a Slanting
Bough" painted on the entablature of the front porch of the Hu Chung
Hall. He asked who the painter was. He was told, "a newly promoted
young painter." The Emperor was pleased and conferred upon him
the purple silk for 6th grade officials and the long robe which was a
special reward. No one could figure out the reason. An attendant
close to the Emperor once asked him and his reply was: "There are
few who are skillful enough to paint the monthly rose, for its flowers,
stamens, and leaves differ with the four seasons and in the morning
and evening appearance. This painting's rose is exactly like one
[seen] at noon on a spring day --- that is why I richly rewarded him."

  In front of the Hsüan-ho Hall was planted a lichee tree;
when it bore fruit it brought a smile of pleasure to the Emperor's
face. By chance, a peacock was under it. Quickly, the Emperor
summoned the painters of the Academy and ordered them to paint it.
Each painter exerted his skills to the utmost and the results were
gaudily colored and brilliant. The peacock [in the painting] was about
to mount a pile of cane and had raised its right foot first. The
Emperor said: "Unsatisfactory." The painters were alarmed and
uncomprehending. After several days they were again summoned and
questioned by the Emperor, but they did not know how to reply.
Whereupon the Emperor said: "When the peacock ascends to a high
place it invariably raises its left foot first." The painters were
abashed and apologetic.

  Among the most precious works kept in the Council Chamber
of the Hsüan-ho Hall was a set of paintings by Chan Tzu-ch'ien展子虔 [60]
called "The Four Conveyances." The Emperor loved and enjoyed each
of them. Sometimes he could not tear himself away from them all day.
Regretfully, there were only three (of the originally four) pictures;
the "Moving/or Transport on the Water" picture alone was missing
from the series. One day an official went to Lo-yang; he happened

to hear that one of Lo-yang's old families had it. Immediately, he asked Lo-yang's chief magistrate if he could see it. When he saw it, he said, startled: "This really is the Council Chamber's missing painting." Forthwith, it was presented to the Emperor. As the saying goes: "When Heaven gives birth to a divine sage, all things will finally come to him."

I heard from Hsüeh Chih 薛志 :[61] "When Empress Ming Ta's 明達 [62] pavilion was first finished, there was a picture of "The Hundred Monkeys" by Liu I 劉益 [63] in the left corridor. Later, I painted a picture of "The Hundred Cranes" in the right corridor in order to complement it. In the character of each there was nothing that clashed with the other. In accord with an imperial decree, we were well rewarded, ten times the original sum."

During the Cheng-ho era (1111-1117), each time the Emperor (Hui-tsung) painted a fan, [the members of] the various residences of the Six Palaces competed in copying it, occasionally resulting in several hundred copies. Among those noblemen and close associates, there were some who often sought the Emperor's signature.

During the days when my grandfather was in the Bureau of Military Affairs, there was a decree granting him a mansion in the vicinity of the Dragon Stream Bridge. My late father was vice minister and served as Director of a Bureau. As usual, he sent an Inner Bureau Envoy to oversee the pasting up of paintings on the walls.[64] Academy painters had done all of those works --- of such categories as feather and fur, flower and bamboo, as well as "Family Celebration" pictures. One day my father went to inspect them. He saw the mounter using an old landscape painting on silk to wipe a table. Upon examination, it was a Kuo Hsi painting. He asked from whence it came, but the mounter said he did not know. He also asked the Inner Bureau Envoy who said: "This was discarded from the Inner Storage. Formerly, Emperor Shen-tsung (reigned 1068-1086) loved Kuo Hsi paintings. He had the walls of one hall covered solely with Kuo Hsi works. But after the present emperor ascended the throne, he replaced them with ancient paintings. There were more besides this one which were put into storage." My father said: "I will hopefully request of the Emperor that if only I could receive this [one] discarded painting, I would be satisfied." The next day a decree was issued that granted all [of the paintings] to my father. Moreover, the Emperor ordered that they be delivered to our house. Hence, the walls of our house have nothing but Kuo Hsi paintings. Really, this was a rare occasion.

During the Cheng-ho era, there was a distant relative of the Imperial family with an unrecorded personal name, who was a great collector of rare pictures. Frequently, princes and noblemen asked him to appraise [their paintings]. Thereupon he began to have relations with ordinary merchants (antique sellers). Wherever there was a rare work he would inevitably use cunning schemes to get it into his home. At that time he would make a copy and exchange it for the genuine article, without the owner being able to know it. Then he sold the original version at a high price. In the end, those pictures circulated three or four times (copied and recopied). As a consequence, at that time, he was given the nickname "Thrice Cheap."[65]

Kou Ch'u-shih 勾處士 , whose personal name is not recorded, was the greatest connoisseur of the Hsüan-ho era (1119-1126). As he was held in great esteem [by the Emperor], every article that was presented to the court from all areas, Kou had to appraise. The Emperor intended to appoint him as an official, but Kou declined and did not become one. All that was bestowed on him was his style Ch'u-shih, and the rank of tai-chao in the Painting Academy.

The "boundary paintings" of the Painting Academy [revealed] great skill, and there was a particular rivalry as regards new ideas. I once saw a scroll which was really lovable and delightful. It was a painting of a hall corridor, painted in dazzling gold-and-green technique, with a red gate half-open, exposing half of the figure of a palace lady behind the door in the act of throwing away nut shells contained in a dustpan --- such as gingko nut, lichee nut, walnut, yew-nut, chestnut, hazelnut, and ch'ien-nut --- each kind could be distinguished, each was separated. There exist works of such refinement and subtleness [produced in the Academy].

According to the regulations established under T'ai-tsu (reigned 960-975) and T'ai-tsung (reigned 976-997), all of the tai-chao when beginning their careers had only six classes in which to serve. These were: mo-lo 模勒 (copying, by engraving on stone, pictures and calligraphy), shu-tan 書丹 (writing characters on stones and tomb-stones), chuang-pei 裝背 (mounting of calligraphy and paintings), chieh-tso 界作 (to paint architecture), fei-po-pi 飛白筆

(to write in the "flying white" technique), and <u>miao-hua lan-chieh</u> 描畫
欄界 (the making of sketches ? preparatory to painting). Although
Emperor Hui-tsung was so fond of painting, he yet did not wish ---
just because of his love and pleasure in it --- to suddenly introduce
[new] ranks (or titles). Therefore, those who obtained official
status in the Painting Academy merely had to follow the old system
and were ranked according to the six classes. This sufficiently
illustrates the wise ideas on which [these classes] were based.

According to the present dynasty's old system, everyone
who was advanced in art, although they could wear the purple
robe [6th rank and above], they were unable to wear the "fish-pendant"
(<u>p'ei-yü</u> 佩魚).[66] During the Cheng-ho and Hsüan-ho eras (1111-1126),
outstanding officials in the Belles-lettres and Painting Academies
were given special permission to wear the "fish-pendant." Whenever
the officials of <u>tai-chao</u> rank were lining up according to class, the
Belles-lettres Academy was at the head and the Painting Academy was
next,[67] while the Music Academy (<u>Ch'in-yüan</u> 琴院), and all the
artisans such as the makers of jade chess-pieces were ranked below.
All of those who were of first-degree scholar status in the Painting
Academy were excused whenever they committed a transgression,
and released from the punishment due their crimes. If the crime was
serious, they could appeal to the Emperor for decision. Moreover,
the daily compensation of artisans of the other offices was called
"food money" (<u>shih-ch'ien</u> 食錢), whereas the two offices' [Belles-lettres
and Painting] was called "wages" (<u>feng</u> 俸). Their value, when
compared on the basis of payment, [reveals that] they were not
treated like the majority of artisans. At the Hall of Astute Thoughts,
there was a daily order for a versatile painter with the rank of
<u>tai-chao</u> to lodge there for the night in order to be ready for any
unexpected summons [from the Emperor]. Other officers did not have
to do this.

Those who were summoned to take the examinations of
the Painting Academy were from all areas. They came in a continuous
stream. Many of them were unsuitable and were rejected. What was
esteemed at that time was solely form-likeness. If one were self-
expressive or free, then he was said to be not in accord with the rules
or lacking a master's instruction. As a consequence, what he produced
was mere artisan's work and he was unable to rise.

Generally, the selection of Painting Academicians was not solely because of artistic talent. Often a man's personality was the foremost factor. If summoned unexpectedly there was the apprehension of being subjected to [the Emperor's] scrutiny and questions. This is the reason why Liu I 劉益 , who suffered from the anomaly of a pathological (or sickening) repetitiveness, [68] never obtained an audience [with the Emperor], despite his service as an Imperial Painter. He was disappointed all his life.

The Korean pine fan is similar in form to "rhythm boards. "[69] The natives (of Korea) say that it is not of pine but soaked willow bark, which is why it is soft, glossy, and coveted. Since its grain closely resembles a pine it is called a "pine fan. " Su Tung-p'o spoke of the grain of the white pine of Korea as being straight and spread out. When split, it is made into fans. It is like the plaited strands from the heart of the coir palm tree of Shu. Su Tung-p'o was possibly referring to the [fan of] soaked willow. Moreover, there are (Korean) fans made of paper, whose handles are made from the glossy bamboo used for making lutes. They are similar to the folding fans made in the market-place; but in delicacy and fineness there is nothing in China that can match them. When these fans are spread out, their width is one foot and three to four inches, but when folded, their width is just a little over two fingers. Among those which are painted, many depict the appearance of gentlewomen as they ride in carriages, on horses, walk on green grass, [70] and gather grasses. [71] The surfaces of the fans are prepared with gold and silver powder to attain the sparkle of the Milky Way, stars, moon, and heavenly bodies. They are possessed of a blurred form-likeness since in their arrival from afar they were rubbed and abraded. Those that are stained in blue and green are unusual in the extreme, different from what we have in China; chiefly, they are done in tones of sky blue and sea green --- those done in recent years are still more clever and skillful. There are also round fans made of thin white silk, and which have distinctive handles with lengths of several feet that are unusual.

[Huang] Shan-ku mentions these fans, saying:[72] "The Governor of K'uai-chi 會稽 [73] had a fan from San-Han [Korea] 三韓 . He gave it to me as a present. [74] [The knowledge of] foreign people which come within our view (i.e. seeing the picture painted on the fan) is much superior to [reading] a naturalist's comments about fish and insects. " "Duckweed Beach's courtesans skillfully ride horses. To transmit through words their moth-eye-brows (i.e. the eyebrows of beautiful women) cannot be compared to painting; these precious fans should truly be gathered together with the Ch'en hawk. [75] I have now recorded this on the pared-off tablets. "[76]

       The Wo 倭 (Japanese) fan is made of pine boards a little over two fingers in width in layers, like a folding fan. Its handle is pierced with a copper rivet and fitted with yellow silk cords. It is extremely ingenious. The landscapes, figures, pines, bamboo, flowers, and grasses that are painted in variegated bright colors[77] on these fans are really delightful. The sheriff in charge of Chu-shan District (Hupei Province), Mr. Wang Hsien-hui, a relative of Empress Hui-kung 惠恭 , [78] had once served as Maritime Trade Commissioner at Ming-chou (Ningpo, Chekiang), and [in that position] acquired two of those fans.

       In the West, in Central India, there are the priests of the Nālandā Monastery, many of whom paint portraits of the Buddha, the Bodhisattvas, and Arhats on Indian cloth. These Buddhist representations are exceedingly different from those of China: their eyes are larger, their mouths and ears altogether strange. A cord of the Brahmins runs over their right shoulder; sitting or standing, they are bare to the waist. First, the five mystic syllables are written on the back of the painting[79] and then the five colors (green, yellow, red, white, and black) are daubed on the obverse. Either gold or vermilion is used for the ground. They say that cow's glue is offensive;[80] therefore, they use a mixture of peach resin and water in which willow branches have been soaked, and which very firmly soaks [into the surface]. [81] China has not yet acquired those techniques. When Mr. Shao was prefect of Li-chou[82], priests used to come from India to the public office where they were ordered to paint pictures of the Buddha. At present, in the Tea and Horses Office there is a picture of the Sixteen Arhats.

Notes

1. Chang Yen-yüan, LTMHC.

2. Shao-ling: hao of Tu Fu 杜甫, (712-770), the T'ang poet.
He was born at Tu-ling in Shensi. Hence, he was spoken of
as Shao-ling or Tu Shao-ling. See Giles, B. D. 2058.

3. Some poems by Tu Fu on painting: "Poem playfully inscribed
for a landscape picture painted by Wang Tsai" (戲題王宰畫山
水圖歌). This poem is quoted in Han Cho's Shan-shui ch'un-
ch'üan chi; see chapter titled "Concerning Ancient and Modern
Scholars," note 68. "Poem playfully written about a picture of
two pines by Wei Yen." This poem is quoted by Teng Ch'un
in this chapter (see note 21).

4. Ch'ang-li: hao of Han Yü 韓愈, (768-824), the T'ang prose
stylist. Giles, B. D., 632.

5. The essay referred to is Hua-chi 畫記 ("Account of Painting").
It is no longer extant and is not included in his bibliography.
Kuo Jo-hsü mentions it in T'u-hua chien-wen chih. See Soper,
Experiences, p. 86 and note 664.

6. Wen-chung Ou kung refers to Ou-yang Hsiu (1007-1072), the
famous Sung poet, who was canonized as Ou-yang Wen-chung
kung. Giles, B. D., 1592.

7. The three Su are Su Hsün 蘇洵, and his two sons, Su Shih 軾,
and Su Ch'e 轍. Su Shih (Su Tung-p'o 蘇東坡, 1036-1101)
was the most renowned of the three. Biography of Hsün:
Sung shih (hereafter referred to as SS), ch. 443; Shih: ibid.,
ch. 338; Ch'e: ibid., ch. 339. See also The Gay Genius, The
Life and Times of Su Tung-p'o by Lin Yutang, N. Y., 1947.

8. The two Ch'ao are: Ch'ao Pu-chih 晁補之 (1053-1110), a
painter as well as a poet (see Sirén, Chinese Painting, Vol. II,
Lists, p. 43), and Ch'ao Yüeh-chih 晁説之 (1059-1129), a
bird and flower painter (see ibid., erroneously listed as
"Ch'ao Shuo-chih"). Susan Bush writes that Ch'ao Yüeh-chih
and Ch'ao Pu-chih were cousins, not brothers. See The Chinese
Literati on Painting, op. cit., note 36, p. 278.

9. Shan-ku is the hao of Huang T'ing-chien 黃庭堅 (1045-1105), the
great Sung poet. See SS, ch. 444.

10. Hou-shan is the <u>hao</u> of Ch'en Shih-tao 陳師道 (1053-1101), poet and follower of Su Shih. SS, ch. 444.

11. Wan-ch'iu is the <u>hao</u> of Chang Lei 張耒 (1052-1112), poet and follower of Su Shih. SS, ch. 440.

12. Huai-hai is the <u>hao</u> of Ch'in Kuan 秦觀 (1049-1100), poet and follower of Su Shih. See SS, ch. 444. B.D., 391.

13. Yüeh-yen was the literary name of Li Ch'ih 李廌 , <u>tzu</u> Fang-shu 方叔 , died after 1100. Follower of Su Shih. SS, ch. 444.

14. Man-shih is a <u>hao</u> of Mi Fei 米芾 (1051-1107), calligrapher, painter, art critic. Author of <u>Hua-shih</u> 書史 . See Sirén, CP II, Lists, p. 77. Sirén inexplicably left out Mi Fei's name in his translation of this passage in <u>The Chinese on the Art of Painting</u>, p. 88.

15. Lung-mien is the <u>hao</u> of Li Kung-lin 李公麟 (1049-c.1106), great painter and antiquarian. Sirén, CP II, Lists, p. 60. SS, ch. 444.

16. Kuo Jo-hsü, THCWC, <u>Experiences</u>, p. 15.

17. Chu Ching-chen refers to Chu Ching-hsüan 朱景玄 (early to mid 9th century). Because "Hsüan" was a Sung ancestral name and its use taboo, Teng Ch'un has substituted "chen." The work mentioned is better known under the name <u>T'ang-ch'ao ming-hua lu</u>. Tr. by A. Soper, in <u>Archives</u>, Vol. IV, 1950.

18. Huang Hsiu-fu is the Sung author of <u>I-chou ming-hua-lu</u> (<u>lu</u> 錄 , not <u>chi</u> 集 , as written by Teng Ch'un), with a preface dated 1006. It is sometimes confused with <u>I-chou hua lu</u> by Hsin Hsien 辛顯 , a work which is known only through Kuo Jo-hsü's THCWC. Soper, <u>Experiences</u>, pp. 114-115, note 46, does not come to a definite conclusion about the relationship of the two (or one?) works.

19. The original Chu Ching-chen phrase runs: 外有不拘常法又有 逸品以表其優劣也 . Soper translates: "Outside of this system, (for those) not bound by any orthodox rules, there is an "untrammelled" category, to show their relative excellence." Soper tr., TCMHL, p. 7. Teng Ch'un's paraphrase reads: 逸格不 拘常法,用表賢愚 . It seems that the <u>i</u> category painters, because of their unorthodoxy, were not judged by the traditional standards of excellence. But just how they were

ranked in relation to the other categories remains ambiguous. Teng Ch'un seems to take a more favorable view than Chu Ching-chen, agreeing as he does with Huang Hsiu-fu in placing i-p'in first.

20. The Tu Fu poem referred to is: "On a winter day (in A. D. 749) I visited the temple of Lao-tzu in the northern part of the city of Lo-yang." (冬日洛城北謁玄元皇帝廟   ). See E. von Zach, Tu Fu's Gedichte, I, 38, for a German translation. The poem describes the power of paintings by Wu Tao-tzu on the walls of the Taoist temple. The line quoted is in reference to a painting of "The Five Sages" (i.e. the five predecessors of Ming Huang of the T'ang dynasty). The LTMHC, ch. III, Section 4, also quotes from this poem (though inaccurately). See Acker, Some T'ang, p. 363. Chu Ching-hsüan in TCMHL quotes it (Soper,tr. , TCMHL, pp. 8-9), as does Kuo Jo-hsü (Experiences, p. 43).

21. This is quoted from Tu Fu's poem: 戲為韋偃雙松圖歌 "Poem playfully written about a picture of two pines by Wei Yen." See von Zach, op. cit. , VII, 32. Wei Yen, a T'ang painter, was highly regarded by Chang Yen-yüan for his trees, rocks and figure paintings. Tu Fu is echoing this regard in his poem.

22a. From Su Tung-p'o's poem "Tzu Yu hsin-hsiu Ju-chou Lung-hsing Ssu Wu hua pi" (Su Tung-p'o chi, Basic Sinological Series ed. Ch. 7).

22b. From Su Tung-p'o's poem "Wang Wei Wu Tao-tzu hua" (Su Tung-p'o chi, Basic Sinological Series ed. Ch. 2).

23. Ku K'ai-chih (c. 344-c.406) and Lu T'an-wei (5th c.) are regarded as two of the most venerable ancestors of Chinese painting.

24. Teng Ch'un is referring to his own preface as well as to a passage in Kuo Jo-hsü's THCWC, ch. 1, Section titled "Lun ch'i-yün fei shih" (論氣韻非師). Experiences, p. 15; cf. Cahill, Wu Chen, p. 19.

25. Sun Wei, also called Yü 遇 , 9th c. Considered by Teng Ch'un to be the best exponent of the i manner.

26. Ching P'o, Five Dynasties painter. Native of Szechwan. Resigned from office and lived in seclusion at Mt. K'uang.

27. Quoted from THCWC, ch. 6. There is an ellipsis after 壯觀 , which changes the time sequence and meaning. In Kuo Jo-hsü, a monk named Meng-kuei 夢歸 writes on the walls of the verandah corridor about the paintings and it is his calligraphy which draws the crowd. Experiences, pp. 98-99.

28. Tu Mo, a Northern Sung poet whose verse was extremely heroic but frequently unsuitable as to rhythm. Native of Li-yang. His tzu was Shih Hsiung 師雄 .

29. Lu T'ung. T'ang poet. His hao was Yü-ch'uan-tzu 玉川子 . Pupil of Han Yü. Giles, B.D. 1437.

30. Ma I. Poet friend of Lu T'ung. Both strove for the same spirit in their poetry.

31. Ou-yang Chiung (896-971). An official under both the Wang and Meng regimes in Shu. Also served the Sung court at the end of his life. A poet and renowned flute player. SS, ch. 479. See Experiences, p. 99, for Kuo Jo-hsü's mention of a long poem (which Teng Ch'un derogatorily terms "mistake") praising the T'ien Yü picture by Ching P'o. This poem is recorded in T'ai-p'ing kuang-chi 太平廣記 , ccxiv.

32. Hsin Hsien. Reputed author of I-chou hua-lu. See note 18. Kuo Jo-hsü merely notes Hsin Hsien's words: "Hsing (sic) Hsien, [however], says that the painting by Ching Huan was very far from equalling Sun Wei's." Experiences, p. 99.

33. Wang Ning. Eleventh century tai-chao in the Painting Academy. Specialized in bird and flower paintings. Sirén, CP II, Lists, p. 85.

34. Hsiu-fan. A monk-painter of the Sung whose specialty was painting rocks of the Great Lake in Kiangsu.

35. Liu Chen-po. I have been unable to identify this painter. Perhaps he is the Liu Tao-shih 劉道士 mentioned by Mi Fei in the Hua-shih. A Northern Sung Taoist landscape painter who was said to have forgotten his name.

36. T'ung Hsiang. I have been unable to identify this painter.

37. Hsü Chung-cheng. Northern Sung Painter praised by Wen T'ung for a dragon painting.

38. Ch'iu Jen-ch'ing (Ch'iu Wen-po 丘文播, also named Ch'iu Ch'ien 潛). From Kuang-han in Shu. Active c. 933-965. Buddhist and Taoist figures, landscapes and buffaloes, birds, and flowers.

39. Wang Yen-ssu. An early Northern Sung painter who excelled in demon paintings.

40. Lung-t'u 龍圖 refers to the Lung-t'u Pavilion (Lung-t'u-ko 龍圖閣). For various titles of Academicians associated with the Pavilion, see E. A. Kracke, Civil Service in Early Sung China, Cambridge, 1953, p. 230.

41. I have been unable to identify Chi Meng or the source of this quotation.

42. R. van Gulik, Chinese Pictorial Art, Rome, 1958, p. 187f., translates a portion of Mi Fei's Shu-shih, in which he extols the virtues of Ch'eng-hsin-t'ang 澄心堂 paper. The name derives from a palace hall of one of the emperors of the Southern T'ang dynasty (beginning of 10th c.). Kuo Jo-hsü mentions this "Pure Heart [Hall] paper" also; Experiences, p. 101.

43. This is quoted from Mi Fei's Hua-shih; see Vandier-Nicolas, N., Le Houà-che de Mi Fou, Paris, 1964, p. 59. Li Kung-lin suffered from rheumatism in the era Yüan-fu (1098-1101) and retired from public functions.

44. Mi disparages Li's inability to free himself from the influence of Wu Tao-tzu. Ibid.

45. This is a reference to the work titled: Te-yü-chai hua-p'in (德隅齋畫品 , also called Te- yü-t'ang hua-p'in) by Li Ch'ih 李廌 (see note 13). The preface is dated 1098. Bibliographical information may be found in Ssu-pu ts'ung-lu i-shu pien, p. 733b. Tr. by A. Soper, "A Northern Sung Descriptive Catalogue of Paintings," JAOS, 69/1, 1949, 18-33.

46. Te-lin was the tzu of Chao Ling-shih 趙令畤 , a minor member of the Sung Imperial family and an official under the Northern and Southern Sung dynasties. Li Fang-shu mentions being with Chao Te-lin in Hsiang-yang in his catalogue. The

13th century bibliographer Ch'en Chen in <u>Chih-chai shu lu</u>
<u>chieh-t'i</u> writes that it was Chao Te-lin's painting collection
which was catalogued by Li Fang-shu in <u>Te-yü-chai hua-p'in</u>.
See Soper, JAOS, <u>ibid.</u>, p. 19. Chao Te-lin was also a
friend of Su Shih. SS, ch. 244.

47. Shih K'o, <u>tzu</u>: Tzu-chuan 子專 , active 10th c.; painter of
Buddhist, Taoist and secular subjects. Most renowned for
his <u>i</u> manner, although Teng Ch'un does not rate him highly.

48. Sun T'ai-ku, <u>tzu</u> of Sun Chih-wei 孫知微 , died c. 1020.
Buddhist figures.

49. Kuan-hsiu. Family name Chiang 姜 , personal name Hsiu 休
(832-912). A Ch'an monk. Mainly Buddhist figures.
Sirén, CP II, Lists, p. 29.

50. Yün-tzu refers to Chao Yün-tzu 趙雲子 . Active during
T'ai-tsung's reign (976-997). Native of Szechwan. Taoist
and Buddhist subjects. Su Shih wrote a colophon on a
painting by Chao which Sirén has translated in <u>The Chinese</u>
<u>on the Art of Painting</u>, p. 59.

51. Lu Leng-chia 盧楞伽 or 稜伽 (active c. 730-760). A native
of Ch'ang-an. Buddhist subjects. Sometimes referred to as
Wu Tao-tzu's most important pupil.

52. Tu Ts'o 杜措 (K'ai 楷). Active during Posterior Shu period
(933-965). Buddhist subjects and landscapes.

53. Ch'iu Wen-po. See note 38.

54. Wu Tung-ch'ing. Flourished 11th century. Buddhist and
Taoist figures.

55. Yang Hui-chih. Acker, <u>Some T'ang</u>, p. 280f. traces the story
about Yang Hui-chih and Wu Tao-tzu to the <u>Wu-tai ming-hua pu-i</u>
(五代名畫補遺 "Supplementary Essays on Famous Painters
of the Five Dynasties") by Liu Tao-ch'un 劉道醇 , with a
preface dated 1059. Under the heading "Sculptors, Divine Class,"
Yang Hui-chih is listed. "His place of origin is unknown.
During the K'ai Yüan era (713-742) of the T'ang dynasty he and
Wu Tao-tzu together studied the works of Chang Seng-yu and
were known as 'the painter friends.' (At first) they were both

famous for their ingenuity and skill, but when the fame and
glory of Tao-tze became uniquely evident, Hui-chih burnt
all his brushes and inkstones, and with heroic indignation
devoted himself exclusively to modeling (in clay) in which he
was able to capture some characteristics of the painting of
(Chang) Seng-yu, thus contending for equality with Tao-tze."

56.   This passage has been translated by Sirén, CP, I, p. 216.
He renders Chung-yüan as "In the district of the capital..."
Soper, Experiences, note 516, translates "...in China..."

57.   Sirén, CP, I, p. 216, n. 3, quotes an anecdote reported by
Shen K'ua 沈括 in Meng-ch'i pi-t'an 夢溪筆談 in which
Sung Ti, tzu: Fu-ku, gives advice about this method to the
painter Ch'en Yung-chih 陳用志 . Kuo Hsi must have
attempted similar works according to Teng Ch'un's report.
It is also reported in Hsüan-ho hua-p'u, ch. II, that Chai
Yüan-shen, a Li Ch'eng follower, drew inspiration for
landscape and rock pictures from watching cloud formations
in the sky. Strikingly similar methods of spontaneous
invention were used by Leonardo da Vinci, according to his
Treatise on Painting. See E. H. Gombrich, Art and Illusion,
N. Y., 1960, pp. 188-89.

58.   I have been unable to identify these two men.

59.   There is a nien-hao of this name (Ch'eng-p'ing 承平), but it
occurs in Northern Wei (A. D. 452) and therefore does not
fit the painters' names given in the anecdote. Aoki has
translated it: "When there was peace..." I follow him here.

60.   Chan Tzu-ch'ien. Active during Sui dynasty (581-609).
Buddhist figures and landscapes.

61.   Hsüeh Chih, tzu: Tzu Shang 子尚 . Served in Emperor
Hui-tsung's Painting Academy. Skilled in ink painting and
flower and fruit painting. See T'ang Sung hua-chia jen-ming
tz'u-tien, p. 374.

62.   Empress Ming Ta 明達 . The posthumous title of Liu Kuei-fei
劉貴妃 , one of Emperor Hui-tsung's concubines.

63.   Liu I, tzu: I-chih 益之 . Native of K'ai-feng. Bird and flower
painter in Emperor Hui-tsung's court. Liu I is mentioned
under another aspect later on in this chapter.

64. Aoki, p. 152, interprets 比 背畫壁 in this manner.

65. Van Gulik, Chinese Pictorial Art, p. 193, translates this paragraph as an example of the Sung practice of making fakes.

66. The "fish-pendant" was a pendant in the shape of a fish, worn at the girdle of an official with a rank of red or purple robe. The purple rank's pendant was gilded, and the red's was silvered. Kracke, Civil Service, p. 82, mentions this award, called yü-tai 魚袋 . He writes: "We are told that by the twelfth century almost everybody among the officials was wearing the red or purple of the two highest ranks. In addition, decorations such as the "fish-pouch", appended to the belt, were also awarded. " But, from Teng Ch'un's account, it would seem that the pendant was awarded only for extreme merit --- at least to artists.

67. The Hua-shih ts'ung-shu edition has hua-yüan for shu-yüan and vice versa. Translators have generally followed the Wang-shih hua-yüan edition as I do here. Cf. Sirén, CP, II, p. 77; Aoki, p. 154 and T'eng Ku, T'ang Sung hui-hua-shih, 1962, p. 88.

68. I am indebted to Professor Max Loehr for this translation. The anecdote is reminiscent of Tung Yü's 董羽 affliction of stuttering, as reported by Kuo Jo-hsü, Experiences, p. 69. Tung Yü was also a court painter and was known as "Dumb Tung. "

69. Chieh pan: 節板. Pieces of wood bound together with leather and used as castanets. For an example, see the painting "Chi-jang-t'u," attributed to Li Lung-mien, Sirén, CP, III, pl. 194.

70. I. e., to worship at the graves at Ch'ing-ming 清明 in spring.

71. Refers to gathering of grasses in springtime in uncultivated wilds.

72. Huang Shan-ku (Huang T'ing-chien). See note 9. The lines are two stanzas from the poem: "Kind thanks to Cheng Hung-chung for the gift of the painted fans from Kao-li" (謝鄭閎中惠高麗 畫扇).

73. A city in Chekiang.

74. Huang-men hua-sheng 黃門畫省 is an elegant title for a retainer. As Shan-ku was an official in the Academy of History, this title refers to him. Cheng Hung-chung was his senior officer (the Governor 內史).

75. The "Ch'en hawk" is a reference to a story in the Kuo-yü 國語. A wounded hawk flies into the palace of the Marquis of Ch'en and dies as a result of his arrow wound. Confucius is asked about it and replies that the hawk came from afar because the arrow that killed it was from one of the Tung Hu tribes.

76. Sha-ch'ing 殺青 refers to taking off the green of bamboo tablets to prepare them for writing purposes. Traditionally refers to their use by historians.

77. Yen-hua 暈畫 , according to Aoki, p. 159, is a technical term meaning "to paint with various bright colors."

78. Emperor Hui-tsung's empress, Hsien-kung 顯恭 . SS, ch. 243.

79. According to van Gulik, Chinese Pictorial Art, p. 165, who has translated this passage, the five mystic syllables mean "magic formula written on the reverse of a Buddhist scroll. Each of the vital parts of the body has its mystic syllable or 'seed letter,' Sanskrit bīja-akṣara, Chinese chung-tzu 種子 ;..."

80. Van Gulik's edition reads: 謂牛皮膠為濁 , but the editions which I used all had ch'u 觸 for cho 濁 . Van Gulik translates: "They aver that cow's glue is too thick (for mixing the colours), ..." Ibid.

81. Ibid. , p. 166. Again, the editions vary. Van Gulik's edition reads 堅清 , which he translates: "which makes the pigments durable and bright." My editions have 堅漬 . Van Gulik takes this passage to be a reference to the mixing of colours, but this does not seem certain. It may refer to the preservation of mountings. I base this assumption on a passage in the LTMHC which is concerned with mounting and which refers to a substance taken from a plant called "Boswellia thurifera," a plant which grows in India and Persia and whose sap is like the peach tree's. See Acker, Some T'ang, pp. 244-245, text and note 3.

82. Li-chou 黎州 was a town in Yünnan Province.

MICHIGAN PAPERS IN CHINESE STUDIES

No. 1.   The Chinese Economy, 1912-1949, by Albert Feuerwerker.

No. 2.   The Cultural Revolution: 1967 in Review, four essays by Michel Oksenberg, Carl Riskin, Robert Scalapino, and Ezra Vogel.

No. 3.   Two Studies in Chinese Literature, by Li Chi and Dale Johnson.

No. 4.   Early Communist China: Two Studies, by Ronald Suleski and Daniel Bays.

No. 5.   The Chinese Economy, ca. 1870-1911, by Albert Feuerwerker.

No. 6.   Chinese Paintings in Chinese Publications, 1956-1968: An Annotated Bibliography and an Index to the Paintings, by E. J. Laing.

No. 7.   The Treaty Ports and China's Modernization: What Went Wrong? by Rhoads Murphey.

No. 8.   Two Twelfth Century Texts on Chinese Painting, by Robert J. Maeda.

No. 9.   The Economy of Communist China, 1949-1969, by Chu-yuan Cheng.

No. 10. Educated Youth and the Cultural Revolution in China, by Martin Singer.

No. 11. Premodern China: A Bibliographical Introduction, by Chun-shu Chang.

No. 12. Two Studies on Ming History, by Charles O. Hucker.

No. 13. Nineteenth Century China: Five Imperialist Perspectives, selected by Dilip Basu, edited by Rhoads Murphey.

No. 14. Modern China, 1840-1972: An Introduction to Sources and Research Aids, by Andrew J. Nathan.

No. 15. <u>Women in China: Studies in Social Change and Feminism</u>, edited by Marilyn B. Young.

No. 16. <u>An Annotated Bibliography of Chinese Painting Catalogues and Related Texts</u>, by Hin-cheung Lovell.

No. 17. <u>China's Allocation of Fixed Capital Investment, 1952-1957</u>, by Chu-yuan Cheng.

No. 18. <u>Health, Conflict, and the Chinese Political System</u>, by David M. Lampton.

No. 19. <u>Chinese and Japanese Music-Dramas</u>, edited by J. I. Crump and William P. Malm.

No. 20. <u>Hsin-lun (New Treatise) and Other Writings by Huan T'an (43 B.C.-28 A.D.)</u>, translated by Timoteus Pokora.

No. 21. <u>Rebellion in Nineteenth-Century China</u>, by Albert Feuerwerker.

No. 22. <u>Between Two Plenums: China's Intraleadership Conflict, 1959-1962</u>, by Ellis Joffe.

No. 23. <u>"Proletarian Hegemony" in the Chinese Revolution and the Canton Commune of 1927</u>, by S. Bernard Thomas.

No. 24. <u>Chinese Communist Materials at the Bureau of Investigation Archives, Taiwan</u>, by Peter Donovan, Carl E. Dorris, and Lawrence R. Sullivan.

No. 25. <u>Shanghai Old-Style Banks (Ch'ien-chuang), 1800-1935</u>, by Andrea Lee McElderry.

Michigan Papers and Abstracts available from:
Center for Chinese Studies
The University of Michigan
Lane Hall (Publications)
Ann Arbor, MI 48109   USA

Prepaid Orders Only
write for complete price listing